Are We There Yet?

THE URBAN AGENDA

Series Editor, Michael A. Pagano

A list of books in the series appears at the end of this book.

Are We There Yet?

The Myths and Realities of Autonomous Vehicles

Edited by Michael A. Pagano
University of Illinois at Chicago

PUBLISHED FOR THE
COLLEGE OF URBAN PLANNING
AND PUBLIC AFFAIRS (CUPPA),
UNIVERSITY OF ILLINOIS AT CHICAGO,
BY THE UNIVERSITY OF ILLINOIS PRESS
Urbana, Chicago, and Springfield

Library of Congress Control Number: 2020949598
ISBN 978-0-252-04356-7 (hardcover)
ISBN 978-0-252-08546-8 (paperback)
ISBN 978-0-252-05244-6 (e-book)

Contents

Preface and Acknowledgments

MICHAEL A. PAGANO

The wide-scale use of connected and autonomous vehicles, also called CAVs, is increasingly closer to becoming a reality due to rapid advances in automobile technology. Early studies in this segment of transportation research suggest that a broad introduction of CAVs could deliver important economic advantages via less pollution, crash prevention, reduced travel time, increased fuel efficiency, and parking benefits. Even as the penetration of CAVs into the automobile market evolves, the technology is not fully understood, and many other significant questions still remain.

How will these vehicles change society's habits? Are government and transportation authorities prepared to make appropriate policy and investment decisions? In what transportation corridors will CAVs be implemented? How are automotive manufacturers and suppliers preparing for the impact of this shift? How will the introduction of CAVs affect parking and other aspects of the built infrastructure?

Those were the questions that the UIC Urban Forum examined at the annual conference held in Chicago on September 19, 2019. The theme of the conference, "Are We There Yet?", aptly underscores the demands and interests of commuters, travelers, and the freight sector of transportation. The white papers that informed the conversation and the overview of the all-day event are recorded in this volume as the eighth in the University of Illinois Press series called The Urban Agenda.

The 2019 UIC Urban Forum was cochaired by Cook County Board president Toni Preckwinkle and UIC chancellor Michael Amiridis, and the conference was under the direction of Dr. P. S. Sriraj, director of UIC's Urban Transportation Center. The event attracted nearly four hundred students, community activists, private citizens, government and nonprofit leaders, and others. The opening keynote address was presented by Finch Fulton, Deputy Assistant Secretary for Transportation Policy, United States Department of Transportation, who explained the numerous initiatives and investments taken by USDOT to guide and stay in front of the rapid growth in autonomous vehicle production and use. Following Mr. Fulton's keynote address was the first panel, titled "Would You Buy an Autonomous Vehicle?" The panel was moderated by Jerry Quandt, the executive director of the Illinois Autonomous Vehicle Association. The panelists were Beth Bond, Head of City Development at Bosch; Joe Buckner, Director of Product Engineering at AutonomouStuff; Don DeLoach, cofounder and CEO of Rocket Wagon Venture Studios; Jimmy Lanigan, Director of Economic Development at Mi-Jack Products/Lanco International; and Dan Zakula, Vice President of Technology Business Development at Mi-Jack Products, Inc.

The panel was followed by the conference's second keynote presentation, by Erin Aleman, executive director of the Chicago Metropolitan Agency for Planning, who outlined the challenges of the Chicago metropolitan area, which is the hub of national freight and rail transportation. Ms. Aleman's keynote was followed by the second panel, called "You Think Congestion Is Bad Now? Just Wait!" Panelists included Rocco Zucchero, deputy chief of engineering and planning at The Illinois Tollway; Dorval R. Carter Jr., president of the Chicago Transit Authority; Leanne Redden, executive director of the Regional Transportation Authority; and John Yonan, superintendent of the Cook County Department of Transportation and Highways. The panel was moderated by the transportation reporter for the *Chicago Tribune*, Mary Wisniewski. The conference concluded with closing remarks by Dr. Sriraj.

The 2019 UIC Urban Forum's external board of advisors included the following:

- Clarence Anthony, Executive Director, National League of Cities
- MarySue Barrett, President, Metropolitan Planning Council
- Henry Cisneros, Former Secretary, HUD; Former Mayor, San Antonio; Founder and Chairman, CityView
- Lee Fisher, Dean, Law School, Cleveland State University
- Jack Lavin, President and CEO, Chicagoland Chamber of Commerce
- Toni Preckwinkle, President, Cook County Board
- Julia Stasch, President, John D. and Catherine T. MacArthur Foundation

Conferences that bridge the academic and policy communities are successful not only because of the caliber of research sharing, articulation of policies, and the coalescing of various communities that make a difference in our communities, but also due to the dedicated professional staff who worked countless hours to ensure that the event was successful. These include Norma Ramos, Brian Flood, Ed Bury, Cameron Johnson, and the partnership with staff from Jasculca Terman Strategic Communications, especially Karla Bailey. The event planner and organizer for each of these annual events, Jenny Sweeney, continues to ensure a smooth and successful conference. Finally, Taylor Long, a graduate student in the Department of Urban Planning and Policy, assumed the role of manuscript supervisor and contributed the chapter in this book that summarized, thoughtfully and thoroughly, the manifold ideas and issues that were part of the conference day.

The annual UIC Urban Forum offers thought-provoking, engaged, and insightful conferences on critical urban issues in a venue to which all of the world's citizens are invited.

Michael A. Pagano
Director of the UIC Urban Forum
Dean, College of Urban Planning and Public Affairs,
University of Illinois at Chicago
April 2020

PART ONE
OVERVIEW

Autonomous Vehicles and Mobility Impacts on Transit and Freight

Factors Affecting Adoption, Challenges, and Opportunities

P. S. SRIRAJ

Autonomous vehicle technology has been discussed for the better part of two decades in various forms. The terms *connected vehicles, automated vehicles,* and *autonomous vehicles* have all been used to refer to this paradigm shift. *Connected* vehicles are those that are virtually connected to each other and the surrounding infrastructure so that they can behave and function in a safe manner.

Autonomous vehicles, on the other hand, are those that have different levels of automation leading up to complete automation and driverless technology. Autonomous vehicle (AV) technology is predicted to be the future of surface transportation; depending on how it is unveiled, regulated, and adopted, AV technology has the ability to galvanize transportation in general and mobility in particular.[1] The removal of human factors from vehicle operation could potentially improve safety by reducing crashes and could have a positive impact on the environment by reducing energy consumption.

Much as the advent of automobiles changed land use patterns around the world, the emergence of AVs coupled with clean energy can have significant influences on land use and travel. While the term *autonomous vehicle* is used in general, the National Highway Traffic Safety Administration (NHTSA) designates different levels of autonomy/automation:[2]

Level 0: Human driver is in complete control.
Level 1: One function is automated (e.g., forward collision and lane departure warning systems, blind spot assist).

Level 2: Many features are automated simultaneously (e.g., steering and acceleration), but the driver must remain alert.
Level 3: Driving is sufficiently automated that the driver can engage in other activities.
Level 4: The car can drive itself without a human driver.

BACKGROUND

The automobile's dominance as a mode of transportation in the USA has been well documented. The reasons for this are manifold, starting from population density, sprawling urban areas, and spatial mismatch between origins and destinations within a region, further encouraged by increases in safety and fuel efficiency over the last few decades. One metric that presents this dominance in a transparent manner is the vehicle miles traveled (VMT).

The VMT for the nation has been steadily trending upward over the past several years (figure 1). As of 2018, the VMT was 3.21 trillion miles, an increase of a little more than 2 trillion miles from 1.13 trillion in 1971.[3] This increase in VMT is coupled with the increase in car registrations (124 million in 2017[4] compared to roughly 62 million in 1960). The number of trucks registered

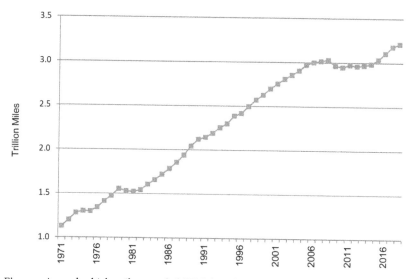

Figure 1. Annual vehicle miles traveled (VMT) in the United States. The VMT for the nation has been steadily trending up over the past several years despite the emerging shared mobility options in the form of ride-sharing, micromobility, and other options. Based on data from the US Department of Energy, Alternative Fuels Data Center.

in the US as of 2016 was about 152 million (compared to about 12 million in 1960, according to the Transportation Energy Data Book). The average age of these cars and trucks is roughly twelve years. The VMT contribution from the 113 million cars was around 44 percent. Thus, car ownership has been increasing, along with the vehicle miles traveled. The resultant impact on daily travel is an increase in travel times. There are various measures of congestion, which are based on the average hours of delay motorists endure. The Bureau of Transportation Statistics (BTS) publishes one such measure, called the Roadway Congestion Index (RCI, figure 2). The RCI measures vehicle travel density on major roadways in urban areas. An RCI value greater than 1.0 indicates an undesirable congestion level, on the freeways and principal arterial street systems during the peak period.

The RCI metric has increased from 1981 to 2008 with only a slight decrease evidenced between 2008 and 2011 during periods of economic downturn. Even with the decrease, urban areas defined as "very large" and "large" have been well above the threshold of 1.0, indicating that travel conditions have been congested and undesirable in those areas. The increase in congestion and associated delays lead to more roadway incidents that compromise the safety of the traveling public. Fatalities on US roadways have increased significantly in the last ten years, to approximately 40,000 deaths per year.[5] This is up from the almost 31,000 deaths in 2009. The reasons for this are many and include distracted driving.[6]

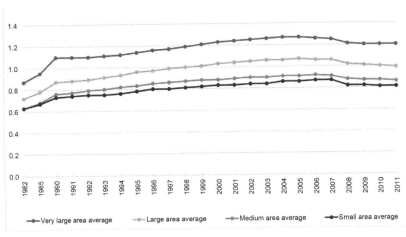

Figure 2. Roadway Congestion Index (RCI). The RCI measures vehicle travel density on major roadways in an urban area. An RCI value greater than 1.0 indicates an undesirable congestion level on freeways and principal arterial street systems during the peak period.

Thus, the current state of road traffic cannot sustain for long. The time is ripe for a paradigm shift in the way transportation is served and consumed. That paradigm shift, according to many experts, could be coming in the form of AVs, apart from achieving optimal modal balance (non-motorized modes, telecommuting, carpools, etc.) that might reduce the inherent gaps in the transportation system.

TECHNOLOGY ABSORPTION

While developing a technology involves inspiration and innovation, getting that technology to be embraced by its target audience is equally important and equally difficult. In this regard, knowing the history of technology innovation and understanding the fundamental theoretical underpinnings of technology adoption will help prepare all the stakeholders who will be affected by the technology. These stakeholders include manufacturers of the technology, public policy makers, and end users.

Human civilization has always been inspired to innovate, and technological innovations have been instrumental in changing many paradigms in our daily lives. Innovations such as the automobile and mobile/smartphones have revolutionized how people interact. Each of these inventions had a gestation period before it percolated to a larger population. This gestation period, which includes technology diffusion and technology acceptance, has been studied by researchers in order to provide a basis of understanding for how society will receive future innovations and what innovators and inventors can do to present their products appropriately. Diffusion tends to be a slow process and varies for different inventions (Hall and Khan, 2002). Predictions of technology acceptance, on the other hand, have been modeled as an S-curve/bell curve or using the Technology Acceptance Model. In a variation of the typical S-curve, early innovators create a product and take it to the market, where it is embraced first by a few early adopters, followed by early majority users, late majority users, and finally latecomers/skeptics, also referred to as laggards.

Through the course of history, personal attitudes and beliefs have influenced the acceptance of new technology and its eventual absorption on a wider scale. Trust has also been found to play a significant role in the adoption of a new technology.[7] In this context, it is important to understand the external factors that influence trust, be it in a positive manner or a negative manner. The literature on user acceptance of commercial products, especially in computer/information technology, revolves around the Technology Acceptance Model (TAM).[8] This line of research broadly argues that individuals' general beliefs and perceptions about technology use help form their attitudes toward a specific technology, and that those attitudes in turn determine their intention to adopt or not to adopt an innovation.

The TAM, proposed in 1989 by Davis, Bagozzi, and Warshaw, postulated that users' intention and behavior are based on their perception about the usefulness of the technology and the ease of use associated with that technology.[9] "Perceived usefulness" refers to a prospective user's degree of belief in a new technology's ability to enhance their individual performance, whereas "perceived ease of use" refers to the belief that the technology requires minimal effort and averts risk. Others have expanded on the TAM by postulating that the intention to use the technology is also a significant predictor of actual use.[10] However, the intention to use does not necessarily translate to actual use due to various other factors, including market economics and resource availability. In addition, factors such as the technology's design, the training and education needed to operate it, and its universality ultimately play a role in how successful a new technology is going to be.

TAM and other such theories provide AV manufacturers a peek into the user beliefs and attitudes that affect adoption. Factors such as the ease of use, as well as the applicability and usefulness of an autonomous fleet for a wide audience, different trip types, and varying geographies, have been shown to play a part in influencing the behavior and intent to use this new technology. The literature has identified two other factors related to technology adoption: perceived trustworthiness of the technology and perceived trustworthiness of the agency providing the service.

While it is beneficial to understand the factors that affect adoption of a technology, it is equally critical to understand the transportation system and the key modes within the system. There are significant systemic issues surrounding each mode and its preparedness to infuse innovation into its ranks. These are presented next for three major modes in transportation.

MODAL PERSPECTIVES ABOUT AUTONOMOUS VEHICLES

The discussion about AVs has rarely been as nuanced as it ought to be. The majority of the literature since 2012 on AVs and the policies affecting them has looked from the lens of a highway mode of transportation and primarily from the perspective of the private automobile.[11] While this narrative is accurate—private automobiles may be the largest consumer of the technology—it still behooves us to deliberate about the potential implications and ramifications of this technology immersion from a modal perspective.

Motorized surface transportation includes public transportation, freight transportation (over-the-road trucks), and more recently e-scooters and other emerging technologies. While all of these are surface transportation modes, they have their own challenges to overcome.

Highway

As seen earlier, congestion on road networks has been increasing, causing delays that are costly to users and resulting in more pollution from emissions. Congestion has not shown any signs of mitigating despite all the investment in road networks and the construction of new infrastructure.

On average, because of congestion, a commuter in a Very Large urban area spends around $1,440 per year in lost time and wasted fuel (figure 3). For the nation as a whole, this balloons to about $179 billion a year.[12] Policymakers and planners have long tried various strategies to mitigate congestion, but some are ineffective. Research has shown, for example, that adding supply (adding a lane) does not reduce congestion because the added lanes attract more induced demand than the increased supply, thereby creating a vicious cycle that is difficult to break.[13] Another, more successful way to curb congestion is through appropriate demand-management strategies.

The most successful and effective strategies have all been tied to parking and pricing. Congestion pricing works to shift a share of peak-hour trips either to off-peak periods or to other modes of travel, such as public transportation or ridesharing (carpool, vanpool, subscription buses, etc.).[14] It does this by levying a surcharge to vehicles entering a congested area or corridor.

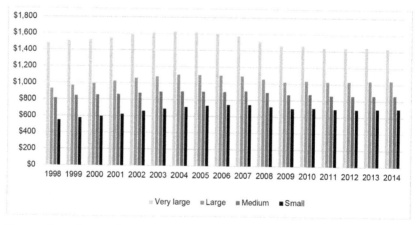

Figure 3. Annual congestion cost per commuter (in $US). On average, in Very Large urban areas, a commuter spends around $1440 per year because of delays.

Various cities around the world have experimented with options for putting this into practice, such as high-occupancy toll (HOT) lanes (also known as high-occupancy vehicle [HOV] lanes), variable tolls (dynamic pricing) on entire roadways, cordon pricing (pricing of entering a specific area or a city in an automobile), and area-wide charges (distance-based per-mile charges on all roads within an area that may vary by level of congestion).[15]

In the United States, the I-15 corridor in San Diego implemented variable tolls in 1998 and has shown evidence of behavioral change (an increase in carpool users) since then. Washington, DC, has used a variable toll since 2017, aimed at reducing single-occupant vehicle use. Cordon pricing has recently been agreed on in New York City and is set to be implemented in 2021; passenger vehicles will be levied a dynamic fee depending on the time of day and level of congestion.[16] The fee, which will range between $6 and $9 per car, is expected to generate about $1 billion in new revenues that can then be used for improving mobility and alleviating congestion in other ways.[17] In all these cases, a significant percentage of the revenues collected will be spent on improving the public transportation options in those areas.

Despite these measures, the impact on congestion has been marginal at best. Over the last decade or so, Transportation Network Companies (TNC) have entered the market as an alternative to private vehicles; they operate on demand in a similar manner to taxis and limousines. TNCs, along with various bike share, car share, and more recently e-scooters, have combined to grow the shared-mobility option in large urban areas and in some cases even beyond. At least as it stands now, private automobiles and the TNCs are possible target audiences for AV manufacturers. However, the market for AVs extends beyond the most discussed automobile version. There are other industries that are going to be affected by this evolution in technology. The two most important sectors among them are the public transportation industry and the freight industry. It is in this context that AVs are poised to enter the market.

Transit

Public transportation in the United States has played a very important role not just in mitigating congestion but also in providing much-needed mobility choices for a diverse demographic including seniors, children, and disabled persons. According to the American Public Transportation Association (APTA), in 2019, 6,800 organizations provided public transportation services around the country using a variety of different modes, including but not limited to bus, rail, vans, and ferries.[18] Of these organizations, 2,229—nearly a third—received assistance from the federal government because they provided services in urbanized and rural areas. The majority of these systems are operating in rural areas.

Bus and rail are by far the dominant modes within the public transportation spectrum, with both accounting for almost the same percentage of trips (47 percent for bus and 48 percent for rail). While automated technologies are already available on rail systems, the bus as a mode is going to be affected most by the advances in AV technology. More systems around the country operate with buses as their mode; buses are present not just in urban areas but also in rural areas. Is the emergence of AVs going to affect public transportation systems? If so, how?

Industry leaders, discussing the scenario of TNCs moving to a fleet owner–operator model and removing the driver partners, perceive that AVs will be detrimental to public transportation systems. This viewpoint stems from associating autonomous technology predominantly with private automobiles. This perception, coupled with the emergence of shared-mobility and ridesharing concepts, warrants a closer look.

Public transportation is heavily dependent on the density of population and jobs in a region. It also possesses the capability to transport more people per hour compared to private automobiles, which typically have had low occupancy rates. A freeway lane can carry up to 2,000 vehicles (approximately 3,340 people with typical occupancy rates of 1.67 passengers per car) per hour, while according to conservative estimates based on flow theory, a bus can accommodate at least four times as many people in the same hour using that one lane, and a light rail can carry 12,000 people per hour using that same amount of space.

At the same time, TNCs and shared-mobility options are emerging as serious competition to public transportation. So far, a few manufacturers have brought autonomous shuttles to the market for use in controlled/closed environments such as airports, university campuses, and business parks. However, there have not yet been any experiments with using these on fixed-route systems in mixed traffic. When that happens, significant challenges are in store for driverless shuttles and AV transit vehicles generally. These include the fact that they are yet to be deployed in actual revenue service. Also of importance is that the transit industry, with a smaller market size, lags behind the freight industry in terms of product availability, technology development, and readiness.[19] Public transportation operators, due to the public good nature of their service, also have to be cognizant of safety issues—the safety of users to be sure, but also the safety of cyber systems. Apart from these broad issues, there are also issues concerning functional elements such as passenger assistance for vulnerable population groups such as elderly, children, and disabled. Driverless systems also bring up labor concerns in the industry. While the trucking system is facing a driver shortage, public transportation systems have to deal with a highly organized and robust labor force. The industry employed 431,514 people in 2017;[20] 96 percent of them were labeled as operating employees.

Of these, the employees operating buses and demand-response services (75 percent) are the ones likely to be affected by AVs in the immediate future. Even if the industry were to use only partial automation to minimize the impact on employees, there will still be a need to retrain the existing labor force to function differently in the context of automation.

Apart from labor issues, other factors are of concern to the public transportation industry. The issue of connectivity to the existing public transportation nodes from the different land uses in the vicinity is one of them. This first mile/last mile connection is an area where AVs can serve as a bridge.

An effort called CityMobil2,[21] funded by the European Union to test the feasibility of an automated road transport system (ARTS), has provided insight into how automated technology can be put to use in controlled corridors as a first mile/last mile connection to conventional public transportation systems. A similar effort called "2getthere," implemented in Singapore,[22] is also evidence of how AV technology can supplement public transportation and extend the reach and market share of public transportation by providing an efficient first/last mile connection. In both of these instances, the autonomous fleet has been deployed in a controlled setting such as a university campus or a business park. While the results of these experiments have been encouraging, there are still several issues that need to be addressed and overcome before scaling up to widespread implementation and acceptance.

Freight

Over-the-road trucking accounts for more than 71 percent of all the freight movement in North America and 5.8 percent of all full-time jobs (roughly 7.4 million of the nearly 129 million full-time jobs). The industry moved about 10.8 billion tons of freight in 2017.[23] These numbers highlight the important role the trucking industry plays in the nation's economy by creating jobs and by being an integral part of the supply chain. The supply chain consists of shippers, ports, and carriers (the trucking industry, railroads, and airlines), as well as intermodal yards.

This important industry does face a significant issue: driver shortage. The shortage has been increasing exponentially over the last several years, and according to the American Trucking Association, it will increase to 160,000 by the year 2028 (see figure 4).[24] The demographics of the driver population

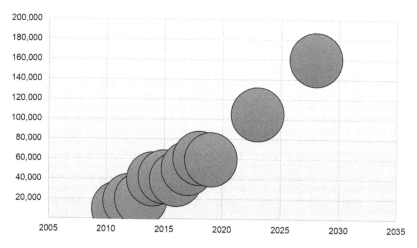

Figure 4. Current and projected driver shortages in the freight industry. Based on data from the American Trucking Association.

by age adds to the concern. Over a twenty-year period from 1994 to 2013, the truck driver population aged forty-five and older increased, while the population aged forty-four and younger decreased.[25] This trend indicates an aging cohort that in another twenty years' time will lead to more shortages as the current majority of drivers reach retirement age and there are not enough younger drivers coming up through the ranks.

The above figures seem to indicate a need to be proactive and ready for a future when more drivers will be needed, which in turn can be the call for autonomous trucks to enter the market. At the same time, many of the studies and projections seem to suggest that a Level 5 automation in the trucking industry is not going to be a reality in the near- to medium-term future. Until then, manufacturers will be improving existing technologies to bring at least a Level 4 truck to the market. A study by Gittleman and Monaco seems to offer the opinion that automation will initially be targeted toward long-haul trucks and concludes that it will affect only about 19 percent of trucks.[26] In the short term, it is also expected that the industry will embrace truck platooning (connected trucks) more than full automation. For example, the state of Illinois has, with the help of an executive order by the governor,[27] begun testing Level 3 trucks on specific corridors in the state to begin to understand the technology's performance and to pinpoint when the on-board driver/operator's intervention is needed.

With this advancement, it is expected that on-board drivers will be able to make the job of operating a truck less stressful and more appealing to a younger cohort. At the current rate, there is a significant need for drivers younger than forty years of age to enter the industry. The use of advanced automation technology may be the impetus needed to attract people to the industry. And if one were to project this trend into the future, even with the assumption that there will always be an operator on board an autonomous truck (albeit with different job responsibilities), it can lead to less-stressful situations and better health outcomes for the drivers.

REVIEW OF FEDERAL AND STATE GOVERNMENT LEGISLATION

Appropriate legislation and regulation are key mechanisms for shaping the adoption and subsequent influence of a new technology that is likely to affect all walks of life. At the federal level, the National Highway Traffic Safety Administration (NHTSA) has provided voluntary guidance and technical assistance to states wanting to test Automated Driving Systems using vehicles with automation at levels 3 to 5. This information has been included in their "Vision for Safety" report.[28] Apart from NHTSA's guidance, the SELF DRIVE Act (H.R. 3388, 2017) and the American Vision for Safer Transportation Through Advancement of Revolutionary Technologies (AV START) Act, proposed in 2017, have been instrumental in providing much-needed understanding and guidance about the testing and use of these technologies. More recently, the US Department of Transportation announced the formation of the Non-Traditional and Emerging Transportation Technology (NETT) Council. The objective of this council is to address any regulatory barriers currently in place that may inhibit the emergence of new technologies such as AV technology.

At the state level, in the last few years a majority of states have passed legislation that will allow them to be prepared to test AV technology and to avail themselves of any federal or state funding to do so. As of 2016–17, eleven states had passed legislation supporting AVs. A more recent snapshot provided by the National Council of State Legislatures (NCSL) reveals that this number has increased to twenty-nine states and the District of Columbia as of 2019. In addition, governors from eleven states have signed executive orders to support AVs in their states.[29]

The passing of this legislation at the federal and state levels has been followed by several strategic and funding initiatives. The formation of the NETT Council at the federal level was mentioned earlier. The USDOT has also announced a new funding program, the Autonomous Driving Systems Demonstration Grant. Through this program, the DOT has provided a total of $60 million to eight recipients for testing and demonstrating the feasibility of AVs. The Federal Transit Administration has developed a Strategic Transit Automation Research (STAR) Plan to facilitate technical assistance to the deployment and evaluation of AVs in public transportation.

The next step in this process is to facilitate this progression down to regional and local governments. The deployment of new technology such as AVs is likely to affect different facets of regional and local travel as well as the associated land use and economy. It is therefore essential to ensure that appropriate attention is given to the planning and coordination between metropolitan planning organizations/councils of government and other local municipal governments as well as with transit agencies. Apart from the downward coordination, the metropolitan planning organizations have to coordinate with state and federal governments so that the overarching goals and objectives of technology diffusion are clearly articulated, understood, and accepted at every level. The metropolitan organizations, in charge of planning for a region's long-term transportation evolution as well as its short-term transportation needs, are uniquely positioned to bring the multitude of stakeholders into this process.

PLANNING CONSIDERATIONS AND PREPAREDNESS

Autonomous technology is evolving at a rapid pace, making it imperative for policymakers and society to understand not just the technology but also the environments in which the technology will be deployed. The impact of this technology is likely to be diverse and far-reaching. Moreover, the effects will be cascading and potentially sequential, similar to the path of a ripple in water. The literature cites the ripple effect of autonomous mobility from different perspectives.[30]

Travel cost, travel choice, and traffic make up the first ripple. When AVs enter the market, they will likely be priced significantly higher than nonautonomous automobiles.[31] Early adopters will start using AVs, possibly causing a change in mode choice. AVs will affect travel times by reducing delays at highways, intersections, and so on.[32] This first-order ripple will spread out and start affecting issues such as vehicle ownership, where people live and work, and the condition of the infrastructure. The rate of the technology's absorption and adoption, as seen earlier, will affect vehicle ownership rates. As the technology matures and penetrates the market, land use changes will start happening due to the impact of technology on location choices. Eventually, the need for certain elements of existing transportation infrastructure, such as parking lots, garages, and curbside parking spaces, may decline. Finally, the long-term impacts on society, equity, economy, emissions, public health, and safety will be evidenced. While AVs are expected to be safer,[33] the impact on overall safety will depend on the rate of absorption and market penetration. Labor will be affected in the transit industry and the freight (trucking) industry. The future of TNCs may also have implications on labor and subsequently on the economy. But these will take time and are the tertiary impacts in the ripple effect.

From a public good perspective, the tertiary impacts, such as effects on public health, the economy, equity, safety, pollution, and energy, need to be in the crosshairs of any new regulations or policies. There is also a high correlation between these impact areas. For example, pollution is connected to energy (source and intensity of use) and tends to affect public health. Historical evidence has shown that "environmental justice" neighborhoods (those with majority Black, Hispanic, or low-income populations) tend to bear a disproportionate public health burden due to brownfields.[34] In a similar vein, these neigborhoods often have significant systemic issues that inhibit their technology adoption. Public policy and regulations need to be crafted carefully with all of these issues in mind.

It is difficult for decision makers and policymakers to foresee the ripple effects and provide the appropriate regulatory framework that will be able to keep society prepared and pliant to absorb the new technology with minimal disruption. At the same time, the evolution of shared mobility and the transformation of public transportation and the freight industry will all dictate how adaptive the frameworks have to be.

Automation in the transit industry may mean that the industry need not be identified or aligned with traditional buses but can adapt to a fleet of different dimensions and shapes. At the same time, automation of vehicles will provide the paradigm shift for the transit industry to begin operating AV buses, shuttles, and pods. This shift is likely to happen when Level 5 automation becomes a reality and is widely tested and accepted in society. This may lead to the growth of microtransit services.

Microtransit is a small-scale, on-demand transit service that can be used in both fixed-route and demand-response settings.[35] Microtransit can either be contracted out (like specialized demand-response services) or operated by a transit agency. Microtransit services may also allow for the transit industry to coexist with the shared-mobility/TNC industry. Advances in technology have allowed for transit fare payment to be more universal in nature. Many transit systems around the world have a universal fare card that can be used not only in public transit but also in car shares, bike shares, and other walks of life. If microtransit becomes the norm, transit agencies will be primely positioned, due to their size and capabilities as well as their understanding of regulations, to serve the role of mobility aggregators. Due to their public role, they can also ensure that the emergence of AV technology does not disadvantage those who are currently transportation disadvantaged. This transformation of the transit industry will be affected by how mobility is perceived and catered to currently.

Two different theories of mobility management exist: mobility on demand and mobility as a service. Mobility on demand refers to the use of shared fleet services for on-demand trip needs.[36] Mobility as a service refers to meeting the mobility needs of the travelers in a region with the help of not just the shared fleet services from the TNCs but also integrated apps that provide a portal for uniform fare payment, schedules and booking, and almost-real-time demand-response capabilities.[37]

Currently, mobility as a service is still in its infancy for a variety of reasons. The TNC providers and other shared-services operators have formed partnerships with transit providers in principle, but those partnerships have not progressed to the next stage, where resources and fare payment are centralized under one portal. It will behoove the transit industry to be prepared to play the role of mobility managers/aggregators in a future involving AV fleets. At the same time, conventional transit modes such as buses are expected to see their own AV versions in the near- to long-term future (five to thirty years).[38] Back-end systems such as dispatching, scheduling, and fleet management are also expected to be automated over the same period.

Planners and policymakers in transit agencies should start thinking about incorporating AV technology into their strategic plans as well as long-range plans for their region. These efforts will help them strategize about capital investments regarding fleet, technology, infrastructure, and other related aspects of service.

The freight industry, which has seen explosive growth in not just vehicle miles traveled but also tons of shipment over the last two decades, is more complex than the public transportation industry when it comes to the use of AV technology. Apart from the obvious over-the-road trucking industry that has been discussed in the literature on AV technology, there is a different need and use for automating other facets of the supply chain. In particular, urban freight logistics is an area where innovation and automation are happening at a much more rapid pace than even in private automobiles. Technologies designed for use in ports, warehouses, and intermodal yards are referred to as *node automation technologies*. Examples of these include but are not limited to Automated Guided Vehicles (AGV), Automated Lift Vehicles (ALV), and Automated Transfer Management System (ATMS). These node automation technologies are being introduced in many ports around the world. The efficiencies of these technologies have been reported to be better than conventional mechanisms.[39] While port-based node automation technologies have been adopted at many locations, the same cannot be said about intermodal yards and over-the-road trucking. Both have yet to see any breakthrough or early adopters for many of the reasons discussed earlier. The industry will need to design and develop training for personnel to deploy these technologies.

The transit industry and the freight industry stand to be affected by labor issues when automation arrives. This is one of the ripple effects of automation, and policymakers need to be working with industry experts to ensure that this ripple effect does not have a negative impact on the economy.

CHALLENGES AND OPPORTUNITIES

The negative impacts alluded to in the previous paragraph are typical of any new technology that emerges in the marketplace. These impacts can be both intended and unintended. It is the collective responsibility of manufacturers, decision makers, stakeholders, and end users to mitigate any negative outcomes associated with the introduction and subsequent adoption of this technology. At the same time, AVs present opportunities to reshape urban form and personal mobility for all of society.

The short-term challenges are as follows:

1. recognition of and safety measures for pedestrians, bicyclists, and other users operating in the same space as autonomous vehicles, including jaywalking, pedestrian crossing at intersections, mid-block crossing, and bicycle use in mixed traffic;
2. the age and condition of the existing road infrastructure (rated Grade D or worse in many parts of the country);[40]
3. the need for AV technology to comprehend traffic control devices, retroreflectivity of pavement markings, and other signs and markings;
4. education and training of the public about AV technology and its use, as well as the absorption/adoption of the technology;
5. job training and skills training for the operators of trucks and public transportation to be prepared for a changing future;
6. liability issues, with a need to craft appropriate legislation and enforcement.

These challenges present significant opportunities for industry, researchers, and policymakers to help make the autonomous future safer, more efficient, and mobility enhanced.

CONCLUSIONS AND FUTURE OUTLOOK

This paper has summarized the various facets in the socioeconomic-political spectrum that have the capability to influence the emergence of AV technology as we navigate the next few decades. History has taught us about the consequences of not being prepared for the inclusion and immersion of new technologies, from the automobile to smart phones and everything in between. This is especially true of consumer technologies that have the ability to influence not just their target audience but also multiple aspects of social life and land-use patterns.

Government has an important role in legislating, regulating, and enforcing autonomous technologies and fleets to protect not just the consumer but also society in terms of safety and sustainability. At the same time, the emergence of AV technology presents the paradigm shift needed to judiciously reshape the thinking about ubiquitous mobility to be inclusive of all modes of transportation. Questions pertaining to the unveiling of the new technology, opportunities for breaking down the modal silos (from the perspectives of funding, service provision, and strategic planning), and so on can be answered through a collaborative approach involving all relevant stakeholders.

Regional issues are aplenty and need a collaborative approach. They can be segmented into those affecting infrastructure, technology, and land use. From the infrastructure viewpoint, there is a need for intelligent transportation infrastructure to enable advanced communications and to preserve right-of-way for dedicated lanes. Other regional issues such as congestion management and signal prioritization may warrant technology-based solutions. Land-use issues such as pedestrian and bicycle facilities in proximity to AV transit routes, enhanced mobility for seniors and individuals with disabilities, and changes in residential or employment land use all require coordinated transit and paratransit plans. Regional planners have a responsibility to understand the environmental impacts of AV from a systems perspective.[41] The regional plans will assume significance based on the rate of absorption and adoption of AVs in different modes.

While it is impossible to predict the future, the literature explores a few scenarios about the absorption of this technology. For TNCs that currently are using a business model of owner-operators, widespread acceptance of AVs will obviate the need for paying these drivers, thereby making the TNCs function like fleet operators and achieve operational efficiencies that will reduce the out-of-pocket cost for the user.[42] This future may also affect how society will view car ownership, leading to more shared AVs. On-demand, ubiquitous availability of self-driving cars may reduce the inventory of privately owned automobiles and thereby reduce the number of cars on the road. If this does indeed occur, the impact on public transportation, and by extension on mobility as a service, will be significant.

In the freight industry, funding grants are needed to test the feasibility and impact of truck platooning (connected trucks), over-the-road trucking, and innovation centers that will further the advances in urban freight logistics. This will allow rigorous testing and evaluation by stakeholders, leading to informed decisions about technology adoption in the freight sector.

Government at all levels needs to be leading the way in all these steps by providing the necessary regulatory framework and adequate funding to test the safety, feasibility, and widespread adoption of AVs across private vehicles, public transit, and freight so that ubiquitous mobility of passengers and goods is achieved with minimal delays and utmost safety.

Notes

1. James M. Anderson, Nidhi Kalra, Karlyn D. Stanley, Paul Sorensen, Constantine Samaras, Tobi A. Oluwatola, "Autonomous Vehicle Technology: A Guide for Policymakers," Santa Monica, CA: RAND Corporation, 2014, xiii.

2. NHTSA, "Preliminary Statement of Policy Concerning Automated Vehicles," May 30, 2013, www.nhtsa.gov.

3. US Department of Energy, Alternative Fuels Data Center, "Annual Vehicle Miles Traveled in the United States," https://afdc.energy.gov/data/10315.

4. Stacy C. Davis and Robert G. Boundy, *Transportation Energy Data Book*, Edition 37 (Oak Ridge, TN: Oak Ridge National Laboratory, 2019).

5. National Safety Council, "Safety on the Road," www.nsc.org/road-safety.

6. Fernando A. Wilson and Jim P. Stimpson, "Trends in Fatalities from Distracted Driving in the United States, 1999 to 2008," *American Journal of Public Health* 100, No. 11 (November 2010), doi: 10.2105/AJPH.2009.187179.

7. David Gefen, Elena Karahanna, and Detmar W. Straub, "Trust and TAM in Online Shopping: An Integrated Model," *MIS Quarterly* 27, no. 1 (March 2003), 51–90, doi: 10.2307/30036519; David Gefenand, Detmar W. Straub, "The Relative Importance of Perceived Ease of Use in IS Adoption: A Study of E-Commerce Adoption," *Journal of the Association for Information Systems* 1, no. 1 (2000): 8.

8. Fred D. Davis, Richard P. Bagozzi, and Paul R. Warshaw, "User Acceptance of Computer Technology: A Comparison of Two Theoretical Models," Management Science 35, no. 8 (1989): 982–1003, doi:10.1287/mnsc.35.8.982.

9. Yavuz, Nilay, Understanding Citizens' Adoption of New Technologies Used in Delivery of Public Service and Information, University of Illinois at Chicago, 2010.

10. Icek Ajzen and Martin Fishbein, eds., *Understanding Attitudes and Predicting Social Behavior* (Englewood Cliffs, NJ: Prentice Hall, 1979); Viswanath Venkatesh and Fred D. Davis, "A Model of the Antecedents of Perceived Ease of Use: Development

and Test," *Decision Sciences*, September 1996, https://doi.org/10.1111/j.1540-5915.1996 .tb00860.x; Viswanath Venkatesh, Michael G. Morris, Gordon B. Davis, and Fred D. Davis, "User Acceptance of Information Technology: Toward a Unified View," *MIS Quarterly* 27, no. 3 (September 2003): 425–478, https://doi.org/10.2307/30036540.

11. Asif Iqbal Mohammad Faisal, Tan Yigitcanlar, Md. Kamruzzaman, and Graham Currie, "Understanding Autonomous Vehicles: A Systematic Literature Review on Capability, Impact, Planning and Policy," *Journal of Transport and Land Use* 12, no. 1 (2019).

12. David Schrank, Bill Eisele, and Tim Lomax, "Urban Mobility Report 2019" ([College Station]: Texas A&M Transportation Institute, August 2019), https://static .tti.tamu.edu/tti.tamu.edu/documents/mobility-report-2019.pdf.

13. Susan Handy, "Increasing Highway Capacity Unlikely to Relieve Traffic Congestion," National Center for Sustainable Transportation, UC Davis, Policy Briefs, October 2015.

14. US Department of Transportation, Federal Highway Administration, "What Is Congestion Pricing?," https://ops.fhwa.dot.gov/publications/congestionpricing/ sec2.htm

15. "Congestion Pricing: US Examples," US DOT, 2019.

16. Gersh Kuntzman, "Report Shows Why the Congestion Pricing Fee Must Be Really High," StreetsblogNYC, September 17, 2019, https://nyc.streetsblog .org/2019/09/17/report-shows-why-the-congestion-pricing-fee-must-be-really-high.

17. Congestion Pricing in NYC: Getting It Right, Regional Plan Association, September 2019, www.rpa.org/publication/congestion-pricing-in-nyc-getting-it-right.

18. Public Transportation Fact Book, American Public Transportation Association, 2019.

19. US Federal Transit Administration, "Strategic Transit Automation Research Plan," *FTA Report* no. 0116 (January 2018).

20. American Public Transportation Association, "2019 Public Transportation Fact Book," 70th edition (Washington, DC: APTA, 2019).

21. CityMobil, https://cordis.europa.eu/project/id/314190/reporting.

22. 2getthere, June 2017, 2getthere.eu/automated-people-mover-systems.

23. Steven John, "11 Incredible Facts about the $700 Billion US Trucking Industry," *Business Insider*, July 3, 2019, https://markets.businessinsider.com/news/stocks/ trucking-industry-facts-us-truckers-2019-5-1028248577.

24. Bob Costello and Alan Karickhoff, "Truck Driver Shortage Analysis 2019," American Trucking Associations, 2019.

25. Jeffrey Short, "Analysis of Truck Driver Age Demographics Across Two Decades," ATRI, 2014.

26. Maury Gittleman and Kristen Monaco, "Automation Isn't about to Make Truckers Obsolete," *Harvard Business Review*, September 18, 2019.

27. Sara Freund, "Illinois Launches Self-Driving Vehicle Research Initiative," Curbed Chicago, October 29, 2018, https://chicago.curbed.com/2018/10/29/18038208/ illinois-autonomous-vehicle-research-program.

28. NHTSA, "Automated Vehicles for Safety," USDOT, www.nhtsa.gov/technology -innovation/automated-vehicles-safety.

29. National Conference of State Legislatures, "Self-Driving Vehicles Enacted Legislation," The NCSL Podcast, October 9, 2019, www.ncsl.org/research/transportation/autonomous-vehicles-self-driving-vehicles-enacted-legislation.aspx.

30. Dimitris Milakis, Bart van Arem, and Bert van Wee, "Policy and Society Related Implications of Automated Driving: A Review of the Literature and Directions for Future Research," *Journal of Intelligent Transportation Systems*, 2017; Deepak Jagannathan, "What Are the Scary Ripple Effects of Autonomous Mobility?" Readwrite, July 31, 2017, https://readwrite.com/2017/07/31/the-scary-ripple-effects-of-autonomous -mobility-tl1.

31. Daniel J. Fagnant and Kara Kockelman, "Preparing a Nation for Autonomous Vehicles: Opportunities, Barriers, and Policy Recommendations," *Transportation Research Part A: Policy and Practice 77*, 2015.

32. Hesham Rakha, "Optimizing Driverless Vehicles at Intersections," 19th ITS World Congress, Vienna, Austria, 22/26 October 2012, www.researchgate.net/publication/291746833_Optimizing_driverless_vehicles_at_intersections.

33. Sagar, Rajat, "Making cars safer through technology innovation," Texas Instruments, 2017.

34. Sangyun Lee and Paul Mohai, "Environmental Justice Implications of Brownfield Redevelopment in the United States," *Society and Natural Resources*, 2011.

35. Micro transit, American Public Transportation Association, www.apta.com/research-technical-resources/mobility-innovation-hub/microtransit.

36. Jeffrey Greenblatt and Susan Shaheen, "Automated Vehicles, On Demand Mobility, and Environmental Impacts," *Current Sustainable/Renewable Energy Reports*, 2015.

37. Kate Pangbourne, Miloš N. Mladenović, Dominic Stead, and Dimitris Milakis, "Questioning Mobility as a Service: Unanticipated Implications for Society and Governance," *Transportation Research Part A: Policy and Practice*, October 2019.

38. "Impacts of Laws and Regulations on CV and AV Technology Introduction in Transit Operations," Transportation Research Board, National Cooperative Highway Research Program, August 2017.

39. Kawamura Kazuya, P. S. Sriraj, and Kevin Peralta, "Literature Review on Automation Technologies in Logistics and Manufacturing Industries," Urban Transportation Center, University of Illinois Chicago, 2019.

40. ASCE Infrastructure Report Card, 2019

41. "Impacts of Laws and Regulations on CV and AV Technology Introduction in Transit Operations," Transportation Research Board, National Cooperative Highway Research Program, August 2017.

42. Adam Stocker and Susan Shaheen, "Shared Automated Vehicles: Review of Business Models," International Transport Forum, Discussion Paper 2017-09, 2017.

PART TWO

WHITE PAPERS

Demanding a Better Transportation Future through Automation

AUSTIN BROWN

The reality: we need to choose the future that automated and autonomous vehicles (AVs) bring, whenever they are ready. That means not asking the wrong questions—like "When will automated vehicles be here?"—and asking instead the right question: "What do we do now?" Answering this question will require coordination between the research community and local, state, and federal policymakers. Fortunately, we already know many of the changes that are likely to lead us to beneficial outcomes: policies that steer AVs to also be pooled and electrified. These are the paths to help ensure that automation also improves outcomes in terms of equity, the economy, traffic, and the environment. Research-informed policies can turn the myth that AVs are our savior into a reality. This paper summarizes the state of research on vehicle automation, with a focus on the potential implications for the climate and policy actions that can lead to better outcomes.

THE WRONG QUESTION

There's a common pattern for new technology as it enters the public awareness. When an innovation enters the media consciousness, usually after decades of quiet precommercial development in the labs of the world, the popular imagination leaps at the opportunity to say how it will change the world. At this stage, the technology seems to have leapt fully formed into the marketplace and appears from the coverage to be ready to go and without drawbacks. This is the peak of the hype. It often drowns out the protest of experts who have followed the technology from its origins and point out the improvements still needed before the technology is ready.

After waiting for a moment in expectation of a technological miracle, the reality of the work and time it takes to bring real technology from concept to market sets in. Now the same writers and talking heads who were heralding the coming of the new technology reverse course and instead point out that the technology in question is far, far, far from ready and in fact has so many crippling downsides that no one could have ever possibly thought it was a good idea.

This inevitable dip is often when the public stops paying attention, and it can be a signal to policymakers that they need not worry yet about setting rules or regulations for the technology since it may never emerge. Some technologies (think the Segway or 3D TV, for example) indeed fade away and never fully emerge from the trough of disillusionment. Others (such as cars and cell phones) emerge and become a real, transformative technology—though usually after more time and changes than originally forecast.

Highly automated vehicles (the sort that drive themselves) have clearly passed the hype peak and are somewhere in the trough. Articles promising that self-driving cars will be here tomorrow have given way to (equally useless) articles saying, "they will take longer than you think." This oscillation between the twin traps of hype and dismissal leads to the transportation community and the public asking all the wrong questions or just throwing up their hands in despair. All this spilled ink tries to answer the question of when these vehicles will arrive and totally misses the point. Some of this problem is imprecision of definition (what level of automation will be possible) and some is imprecision of scale (how widespread the technology will become).

The actual answer is that AVs are already here *and* will also take decades. The nuance is in what we mean by "here."

VEHICLES ARE ALREADY AUTOMATED

Automation in vehicles can take many forms. The Society of Automotive Engineers (SAE) has established a commonly used framework for classifying different levels of vehicle automation, as follows:[1]

- *Level 0 (no automation)*. All driving tasks are performed by a human driver.
- *Level 1 (assisted driving)*. Requires a human driver to interact with one or more automated systems for certain driving tasks associated with steering, acceleration, or braking. Because cruise control is the best-known example of this type of automation, Level 1 is sometimes called "feet off."

- *Level 2 (partial driving automation).* Relies on an automated system to completely perform certain driving tasks associated with steering, acceleration, or braking. Because adaptive cruise control combined with automated steering (often called lane keeping) is a common example of this type of automation, Level 2 is sometimes called "hands off."
- *Level 3 (conditional driving automation).* Level 3 automation represents a significant jump from Levels 1 and 2. At Level 3, automated systems are expected to perform all routine driving tasks, with the expectation that a human driver is always available and prepared to take over if conditions demand. Because the driver is not required to watch the road at every moment, Level 3 is sometimes called "eyes off."
- *Level 4 (self-driving).* Level 4 is the first level that is considered "highly automated" and the first level where vehicles may be fully driverless under certain conditions. Because the driver is not expected to take control of the vehicle under these conditions, Level 4 is sometimes call "mind off."
- *Level 5 (driverless).* At Level 5, all driving tasks are performed by an automated system and it is not even possible for a driver to assume control. Level 5 is sometimes called "mind off everywhere."

Lower automation levels are ubiquitous in cars on the road today. Cruise control has been around for decades, and antilock braking systems (ABS) provide improved vehicle control on slippery surfaces like ice. Since cruise control ("feet off") was introduced, vehicles have been able to automate some parts of the driving task. Many new cars are also equipped with adaptive cruise control and lane-keeping systems that make Level 3 automation possible.[2] Highly automated vehicles (HAVs) are not yet commercially available but are being tested through pilot programs in cities around the world. It is clear that AVs in a very real sense have already arrived.

WHAT ABOUT SELF-DRIVING CARS?

Even restricting the scope of the question "When will automated vehicles be here?" to self-driving vehicles (i.e., automation Levels 4 and 5) does not yield a much clearer picture. Two complicating factors are at play. The first is the concept of the "operational design domain" (ODD). An ODD is the "operating conditions under which a given driving automation system or feature thereof is specifically designed to function."[3] Conditions that may be defined in an ODD include geography, road type, weather, time of day, and much more. It is easiest to develop self-driving vehicles for relatively limited ODDs—for well-mapped areas and major roads in fair weather.

As technology develops, ODDs will expand. It is reasonable to expect that vehicles capable of self-driving during the daytime will ultimately be able to operate at night, or that trucks automated for highway driving will ultimately be able to navigate cities as well. But achieving full Level 5 automation—that is, designing vehicles that are capable of operating independently in any and all conditions—is essentially impossible. Even human-driven cars aren't suited for all possible scenarios. You might need a large ATV to go camping in the backcountry, but you'll find it difficult to steer that vehicle through narrow streets in a historic downtown. Level 5 automation should hence be thought of as an asymptote, not a goal. But given that the vast majority of travel in the United States occurs in urban or suburban areas under non-emergency weather conditions, the impacts of vehicle automation even in early-stage ODDs will be substantial.

The second complicating factor is scale. HAVs are being deployed in small test markets first, usually under carefully controlled conditions. Does this count as HAVs being "here"? Most would argue that it does not. To have truly arrived, HAVs need to be available and accessible to at least a large sector of the public.

The rate at which technology will scale is notoriously difficult to predict. Scalability depends on the size of the business opportunity, the ease of adapting the technology to new areas, and individual willingness to use the technology. This last factor—human behavior—is especially important when it comes to vehicle automation. Surveys show that many people regard AVs with suspicion.[4] This is unsurprising—accidents involving AVs are widely publicized while opportunities to experience AVs firsthand are still few. People also generally show particular caution toward technologies that necessitate ceding a certain amount of control.[5] This is one reason so many people are afraid of flying, even though risks from flying are much lower than risks from other activities we engage in without a second thought.[6]

But as commercially available vehicles become more highly automated, public opinion could change, and change fast.

To illustrate this, imagine that you are a parent of two children. Part of your daily routine is a thirty-minute trip in the morning and evening to drop off and pick up your kids at school, plus an ever-changing array of activities spread all over town. If surveyed and asked "would you trust an AV to drive your kids around," you would probably (like the vast majority of people today) immediately answer "no way." Let's further speculate that you have an oddball next-door neighbor whose kids go the same school as yours. This neighbor decides to be a first subscriber to an automated school and soccer shuttle, which picks their kids up to take them to parent-approved destinations. At first this neighbor seems like an idiot to take such a risk and you feel content in your caution. Now imagine that every single school day for the next six months you drag yourself out of bed to shuffle your kids into the car to shuttle them back and forth, and each of these days you see the smug neighbor sitting on their porch, sipping coffee, and enjoying their extra half-hour of precious free time. Would that change how you feel? I don't know. And, I would argue, you probably don't know either. Attitudes toward new technology are just unknowable before we see how people actually react and how the technology proceeds. If the technology is developed to be safe enough to eventually succeed, there will be early avenues (such as shared fleets) that will increase exposure and eventually comfort with AVs. This "neighbor effect" has long been described in technologies such as electric vehicles.[7]

If surveys can't tell us how slow or fast the transition will be, we are left to look at past innovations as models. Unfortunately, this turns out to be little help. While several IT innovations like smart phones have transformed markets in less than a decade, automotive technology tends to take decades to penetrate even the new vehicle market.[8] As mentioned earlier, people also show particular caution regarding technologies that necessitate them giving up a certain amount of control. Since HAVs are all of these—both automotive and IT, and requiring ceding of control—any estimate of the timeframe for large-scale adoption would be little better than a guess. Indeed, almost all credible studies of the impacts of automation explicitly avoid estimating when the effects they study might manifest.

So if "here" means that a driverless trip is available somewhere in some circumstances, AVs are already here. If it means that a driverless trip is available for anyone, anywhere, at any time, the timescale is unknown and unknowable. It depends on a complex interplay of technological, human, and business factors. If the question is when highly automated mobility will be widespread, the literature is sparse, mostly nonacademic, and totally divergent: industry research by Deloitte, IHS Markit, Fehr and Peers, and Boston Consulting Group provide widely varying estimates of how many miles will be automated by 2030.[9] The good news is that the question of when is not very important compared to the right question.

THE RIGHT QUESTION

Where does this all leave us? It leaves us knowing that we shouldn't ask, "When will automated vehicles be here?"—they already are. It also leaves us knowing that we shouldn't ask, "When will fully self-driving vehicles be here?"—they likely will never be, at least not in the sense of vehicles capable of operating entirely independently under any conditions. Our effort is wasted by thinking too much about the exact timeline along which AVs will develop. Rather, we should ask, "What can be done to prepare for AVs whenever and however they come?"

Answering this question requires a close look at the potential effects of AVs, both positive and negative. Automation could

- make goods cheaper by cutting down on labor needed for shipping;
- decrease emissions from the transportation sector by ensuring that vehicles are driven as efficiently as possible;
- free up time that people currently spend driving to work and other destinations for other uses; and
- dramatically improve transportation safety.

But automation could also

- increase congestion and transportation emissions by making travel by vehicle easier and more comfortable;
- undermine local businesses by encouraging vehicle travel over foot traffic; and
- cause large-scale, rapid layoffs of bus drivers, rideshare drivers, truck drivers, and other drivers-for-hire.

As HAVs scale, it is also unclear to what extent they will be deployed as electric vehicles. Electric vehicles have lower operating costs due to cheaper fuel and maintenance, but recharging time means less revenue, and longer-range vehicles will cost more to purchase up front. HAVs will also have significant electrical requirements for onboard computing, which would reduce the range of electric vehicles and represent a significant energy use.[10]

Since 2014, several studies have attempted to quantify the possible impacts on energy use.[11] The finding from each of these research efforts is that the impacts may be very large, could be positive or negative, and depend primarily on questions of human behavior.

HUMAN QUESTIONS

It's hard to predict which of these effects will dominate in an AV future since they depend on how humans interact with a technology that doesn't yet exist at scale. One particular risk stems from the fact that policymakers are generally not yet setting rules for HAV use, waiting instead for deployment.

The risk involved in the lack of rules can be understood by thinking about how people react to being told that something they think of as "free" is not. There seems to be a psychological switch that flips, leading to disproportionate objections to the policy change. A few illustrative examples:

PLASTIC BAGS   Plastic grocery bags are usually given out free to customers but cause massive pollution problems in waterways and environments. One demonstrated method to reduce use of single-use bags is to put a small price on them (often 5 or 10 cents). Even this small price signals to shoppers to skip the bag for small purchases or to bring their own reusable bags for larger trips. In many markets, however, when these fees are proposed, negative reaction is swift and intense, far out of rational proportion to the scale of the tax.

LUGGAGE FEES   Checked baggage is not free to airlines—they pay for the fuel of the extra weight and can't use the space for paying freight. For decades most airlines did not charge for one or more checked bags per passenger. This made it feel free to the customers, so when airlines began to charge, it led to widespread outrage.

PARKING   Parking is never actually free.[12] For example, a store that builds and maintains a parking lot must recover those costs through higher prices on goods sold. Anyone who shops at that store but doesn't use the parking lot is therefore effectively paying for the parking of drivers in a cross-subsidy. Similarly, many cities pay for free parking facilities out of tax revenues, essentially subsidizing drivers. Although this is well known to the research community, that does not blunt the fury that results when a city tries to set an appropriate price for parking. Residents just seem to "know" that the proper price is zero, and any efforts to the contrary will meet huge resistance.

So we see, over and over, that the psychology of "free" means that it is much, much harder to add an appropriate price to a service once people have come to experience it as something that is, and thus "should" be, free. If we as a society wait to set reasonable prices until after HAVs are widespread, setting reasonable prices will become more challenging.

The default state is that access to most roadways, curbs, and land is free, and pollution is unpriced. Congestion is a major externality—every additional car makes the delays worse for everyone. Assessment of the possible futures and impacts can help show why allowing HAVs to become the next free externality is a risk we can't afford to take.

To get a sense of what's at stake, consider two possible scenarios for a hypothetical person named Robin. Robin has a good job in a major city center, wants to live in a place with a strong sense of community, and values access to culture, services, and friends.

SCENARIO 1: A HAPPY BALANCE

In the first scenario, Robin chooses to live in the city center near their job. Housing is pricey, but the transportation savings are worth it. To get around town, they subscribe to a "mobility as a service" company that provides access to a variety of on-demand transportation options. Robin mostly uses the transit part of their subscription for near-free access to work. Occasionally, in bad weather or when the transit system is delayed, Robin pays a premium to commute via a shared electric AV instead. Because the service knows Robin's destination, it can always bring a vehicle with more than enough range. Robin also uses shared AVs to meet friends and for errands, though most of their shopping is done online and shows up in the middle of the night via automated last-mile delivery vehicles. These shared AVs are all electric and can be easily recharged at stations sprinkled around the city. A few times a year, Robin uses their service subscription to rent a dedicated vehicle for a road trip.

SCENARIO 2: ADVERSE CONSEQUENCES REIGN

In the second scenario, Robin lives far from the city due to high housing costs and a desire for more personal space. In order to manage their commute, Robin purchases a HAV for personal use. They select a model that is powered by an internal combustion engine—the electric model doesn't have the range to accommodate their long commute—and large enough for road trips with friends. The HAV is expensive, and Robin knows that fuel costs will be hefty, but hey, they're saving money on housing. A typical day for Robin involves waking up early and settling into their HAV for the hour-long ride to work. For the first 45 miles, the HAV whips along at more than 100 MPH, carefully monitoring the environment and traffic conditions for safe operation. Of course, there is no avoiding air resistance, and the large vehicle burns through energy as it barrels along. Closer to the city, traffic slows to a crawl. A mix of automated and human-driven vehicles snarls the highway. Robin, dozing through a movie inside the HAV, notices none of this. Once at the office, Robin tints the window and changes into work clothes. City parking is expensive, so after Robin leaves, the HAV navigates itself through the congested roads to a massive parking lot outside city limits. The HAV, programmed with Robin's calendar, returns at the end of the workday to drive Robin from the office to happy hour with friends nearby. Rather than go all the way back to the parking lot, the HAV loiters nearby wherever it can find space. This saves Robin money but makes the already crowded streets even tougher to get around.

Both of these futures provide great transportation service for Robin and result in similar total out-of-pocket costs for housing and transportation combined. But these scenarios differ considerably when it comes to effects on others and on the environment. In scenario 1, vehicle electrification and sharing are widespread. Subscribing to a "mobility as a service" company enables vehicles to be appropriately matched to users depending on the specific needs of different trips. Robin has all of their transportation needs with fewer miles, less impact on traffic, and dramatically lower emissions. In scenario 2, Robin's travel has profound negative impacts on others. The longer trips and higher vehicle speeds generate much higher total emissions. Those who can't afford to own AVs are stuck in the traffic that AVs help create, but without enjoying the benefits that AVs can provide.

WHICH SCENARIO IS MOST LIKELY?

Multiple factors will determine whether vehicle automation yields a world more like scenario 1 or a world more like scenario 2. These include the following:

EASE OF TRAVEL   AVs decrease the opportunity cost of travel time by making travel less unpleasant and allowing riders who would have been drivers to engage in other tasks, both for work and leisure. It's clear from decades of research that the time it takes to travel is a major, if not the major, limiting factor on driving. It is also clear that not all travel is perceived as equally costly, as factors like comfort, certainty, and perceived safety affect the effective "cost" from a choice perspective.

Researchers have found that even lower levels of vehicle automation (studied with Tesla's Level 2+ automated highway driving system) correlate with increased vehicle miles traveled (VMT).[13] Because HAVs are not yet available, researchers have to get more creative to estimate their possible effects on driving. They found that giving individuals 24/7 access to a chauffeur (meant to simulate the on-demand, "mind off" service of a HAV) caused those individuals to increase travel significantly.[14] This seems obvious—reduce the cost or hassle of an activity and people will do more of it. But the implications for transportation systems should not be overlooked. These findings can also provide direction for policymakers. While much policy focuses on financial incentives for positive behavior, a powerful tool in transportation is to give time preference for the preferred mode. The most widespread example of this so far is bus rapid transit, where dedicated lanes can enable buses to provide faster service than driving.

TRAVEL COMFORT   A core determinant of which scenario automation will bring is whether people mostly continue to own personal vehicles or transition to shared fleets. Many users value the privacy and feeling of security of having their own vehicles and may prefer to buy or ride in a vehicle with extensive comfort features. Smart design for shared vehicles may be able to help mitigate some points of resistance by providing a comfortable, secure, and appealing experience.[15]

PRICING   For privately owned vehicles, the bulk of transportation costs are paid up front (i.e., when the vehicle is purchased). For shared vehicles, transportation costs are paid "as you go" (i.e., on a per-ride basis). Behavioral science shows that the more obvious the cost of a transaction is, the greater the impact it will have on a consumer's decisions.[16] (This is why people have no problem swiping a credit card to buy a coffee but think twice when they have to pay in cash.) Shifting to a shared-service model may therefore help reduce vehicle miles traveled, even if the per-trip cost of shared rides is actually lower than the per-trip cost of rides taken in privately owned vehicles (especially expensive HAVs).

AUTOMATION ALGORITHMS   Many of the best outcomes of automation assume that AVs can and will "work together." Vehicle-to-vehicle communications could enable AVs to smooth the flow of traffic, increase vehicle throughput, and merge in a way that does not create traffic jams downstream. But if even a small share of vehicles prioritize the trip of their occupant over the function of the system, these benefits will be lost.

Consider a congested exit lane from a highway. The prosocial behavior, followed by most (though certainly not all) drivers in the United States, is to get in the exit lane early and wait one's turn. This leaves the main travel lanes clear (except for the occasional line cutter), so those not exiting are able to travel smoothly. The most time-optimizing choice for an individual driver, though, is to remain in the travel lanes as long as possible and then merge at the last second. This seems unfair and also adds system inefficiency since if more than a small percent do so it will cause congestion in the travel lanes as more and more people wait to merge late. Most people don't do this simply because of social norms, and transportation is filled with other norms that help keep things more fair and efficient than they would be otherwise. However, if you ask people how they want a self-driving car to behave, they mostly want it to look out primarily for the occupant. If you ask a self-driving car to time-optimize a trip for the occupant, it will make very different choices than if you ask it to help optimize the system. It all depends on what the system is asked to use at its goal function.

PUBLIC POLICY IS HOW SOCIETY INFLUENCES OUTCOMES

The potential impacts from high levels of vehicle automation are huge and uncertain. In most cases we don't even know which direction—net benefits or net harm—these impacts will go. Consider transit. HAVs could complement and strengthen public transit by providing first- and last-mile service to and from transit hubs. But HAVs could also undermine public transit by providing a comfortable alternative for those who can afford it, creating a downward spiral that results in much poorer transit service for those who can't.

Thoughtful policy strategies can help increase the likelihood of positive outcomes while minimizing adverse effects.

Policy has a bad reputation among technologists and technology companies. Legislators are often seen as disconnected from the realities of new technology. Regulators are seen as slow-moving bureaucrats who would rather stifle innovation than deal with new opportunities. And transportation planners in particular are perceived to be perfectly happy with a status quo that preserves their jobs but perpetuates a broken transportation system.

Part of the perception problem is that in many cases, good public policy means that most people never even notice it. Humans are predisposed to notice and remember when things go wrong. We all complain when our power goes out but don't often take time to appreciate the vast majority of the time when it is working just fine. People should certainly demand high performance from public officials. But labeling all public officials as incompetent or corrupt means that the conversation is over before it's begun.

We cannot afford to shut down policy conversations. Public policy is the strongest tool society has to steer new technologies toward positive outcomes. It's also important to recognize that it will become much harder to implement smart policies as vehicle automation technology matures. Right now, there are no individual owners of HAVs to advocate for or against certain policies out of self-interest. Adopting a "wait and see" attitude toward AV technology would mean that by the time policymakers attempt to set rules, an influential constituency of HAV owners and companies will have emerged and could push back.

An AV future that works for all will depend on our collective willingness to take the following policy steps:[17]

1. Set firm and measurable priorities.
2. Establish clear governance structures (i.e., specify who is responsible for what aspect[s] of policy).
3. Implement flexible policy frameworks that can adapt to unforeseen challenges and opportunities.
4. Encourage continual improvement by supporting competition, maintaining transparency, and periodically reviewing and updating policies.

SET PRIORITIES

The first step for policymakers at all levels of government is to clearly define transportation priorities. Some policies will be community-specific, but many will be shared. Some top shared transportation priorities are improved safety, equity, and public health while reducing congestion and emissions.

SAFETY   Safety is the most commonly cited goal for vehicle automation—understandably, given that more than thirty thousand people are killed in traffic collisions each year in the United States and that well over 90 percent of traffic incidents are caused by human error.[18] Policymakers must decide how safe is safe enough. It seems reasonable to insist that AVs be at least as safe as human-driven vehicles. Should even more stringent standards be applied?

EQUITY   Our current transportation system is deeply inequitable, in part because infrastructure has been built over many decades to best serve economically and socially privileged groups.[19] Public transit is the most common avenue through which communities try to improve transportation equity. AV could also improve equity—for instance, by helping connect existing transit systems. But if AVs erode transit, equity could suffer further.

CONGESTION   Americans waste billions of dollars annually in fuel and time stuck in traffic.[20] As cities have grown and become more car-dependent, congestion has increased to the point where it is the top transportation complaint in many communities. AVs have the potential to improve congestion by decreasing car dependence and improving system efficiency, but this benefit could easily be overwhelmed by increased VMT and noncooperative behavior.

HEALTH   Internal combustion engine vehicles emit particulates and gases that pollute local air, causing health problems and shortening lifespans.[21] Transportation is also linked to other aspects of health. How we use land and how we design infrastructure determines how easy it is for people to pursue active transportation modes such as walking and bicycling. Automation could reduce active transportation if it makes travel very cheap and easy, or it could support active transportation by enabling reclamation of public space currently dedicated to highways and parking lots for more active use.

EMISSIONS   Transportation is the top emitter of greenhouse gas emissions in the United States.[22] Reductions of at least 80 percent in the transportation sector will be essential if we are to avoid the worst impacts of climate change. Yet emissions from the transportation sector have remained high as internal combustion engine vehicles remain king and transportation demand has increased.

Research suggests that the only way to see improvement across all of these domains is to couple vehicle automation with vehicle sharing and electrification.[23] Sharing can improve equity and economic outcomes and is the only way to reduce congestion. Electrification is essential for avoiding catastrophic climate change. Policymakers generally should prioritize strategies that integrate shared, automated, and electric transportation solutions. The extent to which individual policymakers prioritize other outcomes will depend on the specific needs of their constituencies.

ESTABLISH CLEAR GOVERNANCE STRUCTURES

In the United States, the federal government is responsible for regulating vehicle safety (e.g., by setting and enforcing vehicle standards) while state governments oversee insurance requirements, liability, rules of the road, and driver licensing. HAVs complicate this division of governance by blurring the line between car and driver. Governance needs to be redefined for the HAV era so that federal and state rules do not conflict. Clear governance structures are also needed to support interoperability of HAVs across jurisdictional boundaries (e.g., permitting HAVs registered in one state to operate in another) without compromising the autonomy of state and local governments.

IMPLEMENT FLEXIBLE FRAMEWORKS

Policymakers should avoid being overly prescriptive wherever possible. The more specifically a law or regulation is written, the more likely it is to constrain technological evolution. Policies should be frameworks that guide vehicle automation toward socially beneficial goals while maintaining space for creativity and adaptation. Successful frameworks will also balance the need for long-term stability with the need for policies to respond to changing conditions. A way to achieve this balance is by establishing set intervals (e.g., every five years) at which policies will be evaluated and updated.

ENCOURAGE CONTINUAL IMPROVEMENT

Policymakers can encourage continual improvement by supporting competition, maintaining transparency, periodically reviewing and updating policies, and supporting state and local action on their transportation goals. Let's consider each of these in turn.

COMPETITION   The US auto market does not favor robust competition. A strict regulatory environment for automakers creates enormous barriers to entry. When Tesla went public in 2010, it was the first US automaker to do so in seventy-five years. The advent of a new era in transportation is an opportunity for policymakers to consider how to make it easier for new and innovative companies to break into the auto market.

TRANSPARENCY   Rules for AVs will affect multiple stakeholder groups. Policymakers should keep public interest top of mind but also take into account the perspectives of automakers, technology companies, transportation experts, social interest groups, and local communities.

PERIODIC POLICY REVIEW   Because of the newness of HAVs, it is impossible to set exactly the right policy in advance of widespread deployment. Policy tools should be built that require regular executive review and changes based on clearly stated principles.

DO NOT PROHIBIT STATE AND LOCAL ACTION ON EMISSIONS   Some versions of proposed federal policy would go so far as to restrict the ability of more local governments to set rules for an automated future that encourage or require lower emissions. Given the importance of climate and health goals to cities and states, any federal policy should explicitly allow states and local governments to set such rules.

Integrate Multiple Strategies

This menu of policy ideas is drawn from a wide variety of discussions ongoing in the research and policy communities, including from the book *Three Revolutions*.[24] It is neither comprehensive nor in priority order. Moreover, no single one of these strategies can work alone—effective solutions will require the integration of multiple policy ideas. These also span various levels of geography and government (federal, state, and local), so collaboration between jurisdictions will be important.

MODERNIZE INFRASTRUCTURE

Conventional transportation infrastructure needs to be updated to accommodate new vehicle technology. Options include:

INVESTING IN "SMART" EV CHARGING HUBS   Simply increasing the number of chargers available will do much to increase EV deployment, especially in high-demand areas. Investing in chargers with additional capabilities—such as on-site storage capacity and the ability to modulate charging rates in response to local electricity supply and demand—will help minimize the effects of vehicle electrification on the grid and will support the integration of EV technology with AV technology and vehicle sharing.

RETHINKING LAND USE   Decisionmakers can support sustainable transportation by incentivizing infill and mixed-use, transit-oriented development; reforming or reducing parking minimums in building codes; setting boundaries for urban growth in order to contain sprawl; and building mixed-use roadways with different lanes for different types of traffic (e.g., one lane for AVs, one lane for conventional vehicles, one lane for bikes and scooters, and one lane for pedestrians).

SETTING PRICES AND RULES FOR INFRASTRUCTURE ACCESS   Vehicle automation will only deliver net benefits for society if coupled with vehicle sharing and electrification. Strategic pricing and priority-access rules are two of the best tools policymakers have for incentivizing shared and electric travel. Options include:

DESIGNATING CURB SPACE FOR POOLED TRAVEL   Curb space is almost exclusively dedicated to parking. Cities could make better use of this urban resource by designating curb space for delivery, drop-off and pick-up of shared rides, and temporary storage of micromobility vehicles.

DEDICATING LANES FOR SHARED TRAVEL IN HAVS   Carpool lanes have largely been underutilized because they rely on planning in advance to share a ride with people you already know. There is greater potential for travel lanes with priority access or reduced costs for shared rides to succeed when it comes to mobility services because the benefits of these lanes can influence travel decisions in the moment. For instance, users of app-based mobility services would easily be able to see when a pooled ride will be faster or cheaper than a solo ride.

IMPLEMENTING DECONGESTION PRICING   Policies that require people to pay to drive in the most crowded parts of a city have been demonstrated effective at reducing single-occupant trips. Decongestion pricing can also be used to incentivize cleaner vehicles by reducing fees charged to EVs.

SHIFTING FROM GAS TAXES TO MILEAGE-BASED FEES   As more vehicles become electric or more fuel-efficient, gas taxes are becoming a less reliable source of transportation funding. An alternative is to shift from gas taxes to fees charged based on miles traveled. This would disincentivize excessive driving while also putting more of the burden of paying for transportation infrastructure on those who use it most. Policymakers exploring mileage-based fees should consider reducing fee rates for shared travel (e.g., calculating fees based on person-miles traveled rather than vehicle-miles traveled).

RESTRICTING OR PRICING EMPTY MILES   The average occupancy of vehicles in the United State is already disappointingly low. Automation could make this even worse by allowing empty vehicles to roam the streets looking for a fare or avoiding paying for parking. We already see that for transportation network companies, a significant portion of mileage is zero-occupant, both between fares and rebalancing to try to find a good fare. Local policy could restrict the amount or price empty miles to discourage excess passengerless travel.

UPDATE AND IMPLEMENT LEGISLATION

Update Existing Legislation

Existing legislation can be updated to support deployment of shared, automated, and electric vehicles. Options include updating standards for fuel economy and emissions—for example:

UPDATE VEHICLE STANDARDS TO REFLECT REAL-WORLD CONDITIONS AND VEHICLE SHARING   The United States has federal and (at the time of this writing) state standards that require vehicles to become increasingly fuel-efficient and emit fewer greenhouse gases. Compliance is generally evaluated based on controlled tests rather than real-world conditions. This is problematic given that human driving is rarely perfect—humans drive at above-optimal speeds, accelerate and brake more than necessary, and so on. AVs, by contrast, achieve operational efficiencies much closer to theoretical maxima. Updating Corporate Average Fuel Economy and greenhouse gas standards to reflect real-world performance would reward the efficiency advantages that AVs provide. Standards could also be updated to provide bonus credits for vehicles associated with a demonstrated increase in pooled rides—that is, if a service could show it had higher occupancy than average, it could have a higher "effective MPG." A version of this approach is being tried in California, which is setting first-of-kind requirements for ride-hailing companies to reduce emissions by increasing occupancy and/or electrifying.[25]

EXPAND ZERO EMISSION VEHICLE (ZEV) MANDATES   A handful of states have mandates that require electric vehicles (EVs) to account for a minimum percentage of vehicle sales in those states. As more states consider implementing or expanding such mandates, it is important to remember that not all EVs have equal impacts. Replacing one personal fuel-powered vehicle with an EV has less impact on net GHG emissions than replacing one vehicle used in a ride-hailing service since ride-hailing vehicles travel more miles on average than personal vehicles. ZEV mandates could include bonus credits for EVs sold into fleets for use in ride-hailing (similar to the Maven program being piloted in the San Francisco Bay Area today).

Implement New Legislation

New legislation can and should be established to address issues specific to the AV era. Options include tailoring emission standards, incentivizing EV ownership, and disincentivizing personal AV ownership.

SET EMISSIONS STANDARDS TAILORED TO VEHICLE FLEETS   As ride-hailing services become a greater part of the transportation ecosystem, fleet-based emissions standards will be a natural complement to vehicle-based emissions standards. A fleet-based emissions standard is under active development in California, through SB 1014. SB 1014, now referred to as a "clean miles standard," will require transportation network companies like Uber and Lyft to reduce their average greenhouse gas emissions per passenger mile. One innovative aspect of this standard is that it allows compliance via electrification, pooling, or a combination of the two. Such a standard could easily be applied to automated fleets.

INCENTIVIZE OR REQUIRE AVS TO BE ELECTRIC   There is no guarantee that AVs will be electric. Simply establishing an electric mandate for AVs would be one way to address this problem. Less stringent options would be to impose a higher registration fee on nonelectric AVs or to implement a mandate that makes exceptions for AV classes that would be very difficult to electrify (such as heavy-duty trucks).

INCENTIVIZE OR RESTRICT PERSONALLY OWNED AVS   There is also no guarantee that AVs will be shared. Again, restricting or increasing registration fees on personally owned AVs is a straightforward way to ensure that vehicle automation occurs only in conjunction with sharing.

Collect Needed Data

Including data-collection provisions in AV policy will ensure that researchers and decision makers have the information they need to assess the success of AV policies in meeting societal goals. Robust data will be especially useful when it comes to fuel use and occupancy.

Policies rewarding improved efficiency for automation will rely on tracking fuel use at the vehicle level. In addition, policies encouraging electric driving will need data on electricity use in EVs and hybrid vehicles. These data may be collected by companies, but policymakers will need to establish strong validation mechanisms.

Many of the policy strategies outlined above emphasize pooling. Understanding the extent to which these policies are succeeding will require reliable data on vehicle occupancy. Data collection on occupancy must be done carefully to respect individual privacy.

No-Regrets Policies to Work on Now

This looks like a daunting to-do list, and it is unlikely that policymakers can pursue all of these at once in a widespread way. Cities and states can serve as test beds of innovation by using pilots combining many of these policies together and carefully measuring the impacts. The policies that perform the best can then be expanded and adapted to new areas.

The looming approach of vehicle automation technologies can also be a good reason to jump-start changes that should have been made already. Cities can, for example, start to rethink the use of curbs, parking, and public spaces, which have largely been developed to benefit the private car. Congested urban centers can begin setting prices through automated toll collection for the use of busy streets, including by ride-hailing vehicles, and be ready to adapt these pricing schemes for HAVs. Cities and states can also start to use better metrics for planning transportation systems, including accessibility and equity metrics. These changes are long overdue and will be a good idea no what comes to pass from automation.

CONCLUSIONS

Public policy is the tool by which our society takes collective action to improve outcomes. Many strong forces will make it hard to be proactive when it comes to HAVs. These include the following:

- widespread skepticism as to the efficiency of policy and policymakers in general;
- an understandable worry about the complicity of HAV technology;
- governance structures that were not designed with HAVs in mind;
- significant private-industry interest in avoiding or reducing regulation;
- a general public that is wary of automation in general; and
- a status quo that has been built over more than a century and that changes slowly.

But these challenges are not an excuse for inaction or delay. Vehicle automation has the potential to bring the biggest changes to our transportation system since the development of the automobile. These technologies and systems could contribute to solving or mitigating our myriad transportation problems. Given the climate crisis, the current state of inequity, the health burdens of transportation, the loss of life to crashes, and ever-increasing congestion, a tool this powerful (for good or ill) can't be left to a "wait and see" approach. Positive outcomes are less likely if communities and researchers delay action until the vehicles and services are already widespread. The best time to have started on getting the policies right would have been when we first put cars on the roads more than a century ago. The second best time to do so is right now.

Notes

1. SAE International, Standards, "J3016," *Taxonomy and Definitions for Terms Related to On-Road Motor Vehicle Automated Driving Systems* 4 (2014): 593–98. Adaptive cruise control uses range-finding technology like radar to keep a constant distance between a vehicle and the vehicle in front of it, reducing the need for the driver to adjust speed in response to traffic changes. However, because humans find it very difficult to remain attentive when not actively controlling a vehicle, Level 3 automation is proving to be as much of a behavioral challenge as a technological one.

2. Lucy Perkins, Nicole Dupuis, and Brooks Rainwater, "Autonomous Vehicle Pilots Across America: Municipal Action Guide," National League of Cities, Center for City Solutions, October 17, 2018, www.nlc.org/sites/default/files/2018-10/AV%20 MAG%20Web.pdf.

3. SAE International, Standards, "J3016."

4. See, for example, Ellen Edmonds, "Three in Four Americans Remain Afraid of Fully Self-Driving Vehicles," AAA Newsroom (website), March 14, 2019, https://newsroom .aaa.com/2019/03/americans-fear-self-driving-cars-survey/; Association for Unmanned Vehicle Systems International and Perkins Coie LLC, "2019 Autonomous Vehicles Survey Report," January 2019, www.perkinscoie.com/images/content/2/1/ v3/216738/2019-Autonomous-Vehicles-Survey-Report-v.3.pdf.

5. William M. Klein and Ziva Kunda, "Exaggerated Self-Assessments and the Preference for Controllable Risks," *Organizational Behavior and Human Decision Processes* 59, no. 3 (September 1994), 410–27, https://doi.org/10.1006/obhd.1994.1067; Peng Liu, Yong Du, and Zhigang Xu, "Machines versus Humans: People's Biased Responses to Traffic Accidents Involving Self-Driving Vehicles," *Accident Analysis and Prevention* 125 (April 2019): 232–40, https://doi.org/10.1016/j.aap.2019.02.012.

6. National Safety Council, "Injury Facts Chart," www.nsc.org/work-safety/tools -resources/injury-facts/chart (accessed May 2020); Kopl Halperin, "A Comparative Analysis of Six Methods for Calculating Travel Fatality Risk," *RISK: Health, Safety, and Environment* 4, no. 1 (January 1993), article 4, https://scholars.unh.edu/ cgi/viewcontent.cgi?article=1119&context=risk; Figure 1, "Categorization of average annual fatalities 2000–2009," in Ian Savage, "Comparing the Fatality Risks in United States Transportation across Modes and over Time," *Research in Transporta-*

tion Economics 43, no. 1 (July 2013): 9–22, www.sciencedirect.com/science/article/pii/S0739885912002156.

7. Paulus Mau, Jimena Eyzaguirre, Mark Jaccard, Colleen Collins-Dodd, and Kenneth Tiedemann, "The 'Neighbor Effect': Simulating Dynamics in Consumer Preferences for New Vehicle Technologies," *Ecological Economics* 68, no. 1–2 (2008): 504–16.

8. Environmental Protection Agency, "The 2018 EPA Automotive Trends Report," last updated March 6, 2019, www.epa.gov/automotive-trends.

9. Scott Corwin, Nick Jameson, Derek M. Pankratz, and Philipp Willigmann, "The Future of Mobility: What's Next?," *Deloitte University Press* 24 (2016): 67–84; IHS Automotive, "Autonomous Vehicle Sales Forecast to Reach 21 mil. Globally in 2035," published June 7, 2016, https://ihsmarkit.com/country-industry-forecasting.html?ID=10659115737; Jane Bierstedt, Aaron Gooze, Chris Gray, Josh Peterman, Leon Raykin, and Jerry Walters, "Effects of Next-Generation Vehicles on Travel Demand and Highway Capacity," *FP Think Working Group* (2014): 10–11; Boston Consulting Group, "By 2030, 25% of Miles Driven in US Could Be in Shared Self-Driving Electric Cars," published April 10, 2017, www.bcg.com/d/press/10april2017-future-autonomous-electric-vehicles-151076.

10. James H. Gawron, Gregory A. Keoleian, Robert D. De Kleine, Timothy J. Wallington, and Hyung Chul Kim, "Life Cycle Assessment of Connected and Automated Vehicles: Sensing and Computing Subsystem and Vehicle Level Effects," *Environmental Science and Technology* 52, no. 5 (2018): 3249–56.

11. US Energy Information Administration, "Study of the Potential Energy Consumption Impacts of Connected and Automated Vehicles" (Washington, DC: US Department of Energy, 2017), www.eia.gov/analysis/studies/transportation/automated/; Austin Brown, Jeffrey Gonder, and Brittany Repac, "An Analysis of Possible Energy Impacts of Automated Vehicles," in *Road Vehicle Automation*, edited by Gereon Meyer and Sven Beiker, 137–53 (Cham, Switzerland: Springer International, 2014); Don MacKenzie, Zia Wadud, and Paul Leiby, "A First Order Estimate of Energy Impacts of Automated Vehicles in the United States," paper presented at the Transportation Research Board 2014 Annual Meeting, Washington, DC, and published in *TRB 93rd Annual Meeting Compendium of Papers*, no. 14-2193 (Washington, DC: Transportation Research Board of the National Academies, 2014); Joshua Auld, Vadim Sokolov, and Thomas S. Stephens, "Analysis of the Effects of Connected–Automated Vehicle Technologies on Travel Demand," *Transportation Research Record* 2625, cno. 1 (2017): 1–8.

12. Donald Shoup, *The High Cost of Free Parking* (Chicago: American Planning Association; Abington, Oxfordshire, England: Routledge, 2005).

13. Scott Hardman, Rosaria M. Berliner, and Gil Tal, "A First Look at Vehicle Miles Travelled in Partially-Automated Vehicles," UC Davis Institute of Transportation Studies, Working Paper UCD-ITS-WP-18-01 (2018).

14. Mustapha Harb, Yu Xiao, Giovanni Circella, Patricia L. Mokhtarian, and Joan L. Walker, "Projecting Travelers into a World of Self-Driving Vehicles: Estimating

Travel Behavior Implications via a Naturalistic Experiment," *Transportation* 45, no. 6 (2018): 1671–85.

15. Angela Sanguinetti, Ken Kurani, and Beth Ferguson, "Policy Brief: Vehicle Design May Be Critical to Encourage Ride-Pooling in Shared Automated Vehicles," UC Davis Institute of Transportation Studies, Brief UCD-ITS-RR-19-14 (2019).

16. Drazen Prelec and Duncan Simester, "Always Leave Home Without It: A Further Investigation of the Credit-Card Effect on Willingness to Pay," *Marketing Letters* 12 (2001): 5–12, https://doi.org/10.1023/A:1008196717017.

17. Austin Brown, Greg Rodriguez, and Tiffany Hoang, with Hannah Safford, Gordon Anderson, and Mollie Cohen D'Agostino, "Federal, State, and Local Governance of Automated Vehicles," UC Davis Policy Institute for Energy, Environment, and the Economy, Issue Paper, December 2018.

18. National Highway Traffic Safety Administration, "2018 Fatal Motor Vehicle Crashes: Overview" (Washington, DC: US Department of Transportation, 2019).

19. Floridea Di Ciommo and Yoram Shiftan, "Transport Equity Analysis," *Transport Reviews* 37, no. 2 (2017): 139–51.

20. David Schrank, Bill Eisele, and Tim Lomax, "2019 Urban Mobility Report," Texas A&M Transportation Institute, August 2019.

21. Mark A. Delucchi and Donald R. McCubbin, "External Costs of Transport in the U.S.," UC Davis Institute of Transportation Studies, Working Paper UCD-ITS-RP-10-10 (2010).

22. US Environmental Protection Agency, "Inventory of U.S. Greenhouse Gas Emissions and Sinks: 1990–2018," EPA 430-R-20--002 (final report published April 13, 2020).

23. Lewis M. Fulton, "Three Revolutions in Urban Passenger Travel," *Joule* 2, no. 4 (2018): 575–78.

24. Daniel Sperling, *Three Revolutions* (Washington, DC: Island Press, 2018).

25. California Air Resources Board's "Clean Miles Standard" describes SB 1014 (2018), the Clean Miles Standard and Incentive Program.

Are We There Yet, and Where Is It We Need to Go?

Myths and Realities of Connected and Automated Vehicles

STAN CALDWELL AND CHRIS HENDRICKSON

Following the 2007 DARPA Urban Grand Challenge many companies quietly pursued the commercialization of automated vehicle technology. Then in 2013 a media fueled race and subsequent hype cycle began that culminated in 2018 with the first pedestrian fatality plunging the industry into a trough of disillusionment. During this same time multiple connected vehicle technologies have evolved, driven by both the public and private sectors. Furthermore, alternatively fueled and shared vehicle technologies quickly expanded in the marketplace.

This rapid deployment of multiple disruptive technologies in a very short period of time has created confusion for the industry, policymakers, and the public about the true state of technology. Now a period of more sober assessment has emerged moving toward industry standards, public policies, and even public adoption of early levels of connected and automated technology. With this early public adoption there is evidence of impacts on safety and mobility as well as further deployment.

The purpose of this paper is to provide a history and current assessment of connected and automated vehicle (CAV) technology. In this paper, we survey the state of changes and anticipated impacts for connected and automated roadway vehicles, focusing on deployment in the United States, and provide some policy recommendations for the future.

Figure 1. Carnegie Mellon University's automated vehicle "Boss" won the 2007 DARPA Urban Grand Challenge and demonstrated the capability of AVs to drive successfully in traffic. Photo by Chris Hendrickson.

EVOLUTION OF CONNECTED AND AUTOMATED VEHICLES

Technology Feasibility Demonstrated: 2007, the DARPA Urban Grand Challenge

While connected and automated technologies have evolved over many decades, the Defense Advanced Research Projects Agency's (DARPA) Urban Grand Challenge in 2007 marked a major turning point in the visibility and commercial interest for CAV.[1] In this competition, six automated vehicles successfully completed a course that required driving in traffic and performing complex maneuvers such as merging, passing, parking, and negotiating intersections. Figure 1 shows Carnegie Mellon University's "Boss" entry, which won the challenge. It is notable that all teams that successfully completed the challenge were US-based, university-led teams. Since 2007, a variety of private firms, universities, and government agencies throughout the developed world have been pursuing further development and implementation of these capabilities.

The Race Begins: 2013, the Second Significant Turning Point

From 2007 through 2013 CAV research and development in both the traditional automotive industry such as General Motors and comparatively new technology companies such as Google (later Waymo) was being pursued aggressively, independently, and secretly.[2]

Then in September 2013 Carnegie Mellon University hosted Pennsylvania Department of Transportation secretary Barry Schoch and US House Transportation and Infrastructure Committee chairman Bill Shuster for a CAV demonstration.[3] This thirty-three-mile ride in a highly automated (Level 4) CAV was open to the media and performed on public roadways at speeds up to 65 miles per hour, navigating connected signalized intersections and interacting with traffic.

Later that same month, Google released news that its vehicle fleet had operated 500,000 miles crash-free with its "Chauffer" system.[4] Google's automated efforts in California were supported by legislation that had been signed into law on September 25, 2012, by Governor Jerry Brown. This California law followed similar automated vehicle driving laws first enacted in Nevada in February 2012 and then in Florida in April of that year.[5] This began an era of states aggressively enacting legislation and executive orders to support the automated vehicle industry and address safety concerns of the public. As of March 2019, thirty-five states had enacted automated vehicle legislation and/or executive orders.[6]

In September 2016, US DOT secretary Foxx announced the first National Highway Traffic Safety Administration (NHTSA) guidance on automated vehicle standards for manufacturers and on policy for states.[7] In the following administration, US DOT secretary Chao announced updates to the NHTSA guidance in 2017 with AV 2.0 and further updates in 2018 with AV 3.0. These updates continued with the framework of guidance for vehicle performance, model state regulations, and regulatory tools.[8] The US Congress has considered various pieces of legislation regarding autonomous vehicles, but none has passed to date.

There have been some limited local government initiatives to regulate AV activity in cities such as San Francisco, Pittsburgh, and New York City. These cities impose guidance or permits, in addition to those imposed by their respective states, for companies to test and deploy automated vehicles on city roadways. Restrictions may limit locations for operations, limit vehicle speed, and add requirements for vehicle operators.

In 2013 numerous companies beyond Google, including Audi, GM, Ford, Nissan, Toyota, Tesla, and Volvo, announced their automated vehicle programs and ambitions for commercial deployment.[9] Much of this AV research had been under development by these companies for many years but not publicly announced until this time.

The year 2014 began an era of industry collaboration, partnership, and acquisitions among traditional auto manufacturers and both established and start-up technology companies. Examples of traditional and start-up company relationships include GM acquiring Cruise, both Ford and Volkswagen separately partnering with Argo AI, and Delphi acquiring Ottmatika and then spinning it off into Aptiv.

To further test AVs in a real-world environment, Uber began the world's first automated taxi service open to the public in September 2016 in Pittsburgh and later expanded the service to Arizona.[10]

Following the Hype: 2018, the Third Significant Turning Point

It can be argued that 2013 began the hype cycle of automated vehicles with overly optimistic predictions and timelines for full automation, which ended in March 2018 with the tragic fatality of a pedestrian in Tempe, Arizona, from a crash with an automated Uber test vehicle.

Following this fatality, the public, government officials, and companies have taken a more sober assessment of the current state of AV technology and developed more realistic predictions for deployment.

Diverse companies and nonprofit organizations are also beginning to collaborate around public educational initiatives such as Partner for Autonomous Vehicle Education (PAVE). This collaboration includes automakers GM, Volkswagen, Daimler, and Toyota, tech companies Waymo, Intel, and NVIDIA, professional organization SAE International, and charitable organizations such as the National Federation of the Blind and the National Council on Aging.[11]

Focus on Standards

Often, existing standards omit or are inadequate for the new CAV technology and applications. In 2016 the Society of Automotive Engineers (SAE) developed the industry standard J3016, which defines the six levels of automation.[12] In 2019 Underwriter Laboratory and Edge Case Research began developing AV standard UL4600, which covers autonomous product safety.[13] Considerable work on new standards and regulations for all aspects of CAV can be expected in the next few decades.

Do We Really Need Level 5 Automation for Success?

Artificial intelligence is challenged in dealing with edge cases, which are impossible to program fully. We may face a reality that some human supervision of automated systems is required for the foreseeable future. Machines are very effective at completing repetitive tasks without distraction, and humans are superior to machines in applying common sense learned through

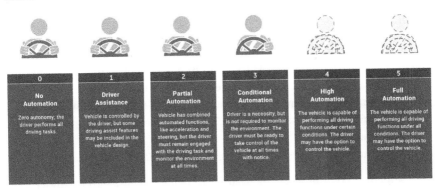

0	1	2	3	4	5
No Automation	**Driver Assistance**	**Partial Automation**	**Conditional Automation**	**High Automation**	**Full Automation**
Zero autonomy, the driver performs all driving tasks.	Vehicle is controlled by the driver, but some driving assist features may be included in the vehicle design.	Vehicle has combined automated functions, like acceleration and steering, but the driver must remain engaged with the driving task and monitor the environment at all times.	Driver is a necessity, but is not required to monitor the environment. The driver must be ready to take control of the vehicle at all times with notice.	The vehicle is capable of performing all driving functions under certain conditions. The driver may have the option to control the vehicle.	The vehicle is capable of performing all driving functions under all conditions. The driver may have the option to control the vehicle.

Figure 2. Levels of vehicle automation originally defined by the Society of Automotive Engineers. Source: NHTSA, 2019.

experience with unforeseen situations. Moreover, Level 3 or 4 automation may be good enough to provide significant safety and efficiency gains, particularly because the SAE definition of Level 5 is a vehicle that "can drive everywhere in all conditions,"[14] a standard that no machine or human may achieve independently but that a machine and a human may possibly achieve together (see figure 2). However, there will be continuing interest in Level 5 automation to reduce the cost of ride-hailing services or freight movements.

Another concern about Level 5 automated vehicles is that they may create more congestion and emissions through an increase in vehicle miles traveled even without any passengers on board.

This section describes the current state and potential impacts of partial automation, or "copilot assistance"; highly automated, driverless vehicles; and connected vehicles. With regard to levels of automation, partial automation would be Levels 1 to 3, while full automation would be Levels 4 and 5.[15]

There are examples of past disruptive technology that was improved over time to where it required less human supervision. Our telecommunications systems began with a heavy reliance on human "operators" who played an evolving role for over a century and can still be accessed on our cell phones by dialing 611. Today any human passenger in an automated elevator system can still hit a "call" button and connect with a human outside the system, but elevator operators were required in each unit for many years. Fully automated elevators were available in 1900, but it took fifty years for the public to become comfortable with phasing out operators.[16]

PARTIALLY AUTOMATED VEHICLES

Partially automated vehicles are now commercially available from virtually all vehicle manufacturers. These systems were first offered as options
in high-end vehicles but are now appearing as standard features on all new
vehicles. In particular, the NHTSA required all vehicles sold after 2018 to
include rear-view video displays.[17] Ten manufacturers have committed to
make automatic emergency braking standard on all models.[18] However, these
systems have varied names and come in different combinations from different manufacturers.

Partial automation systems include the following:

- forward collision prevention, such as adaptive cruise control, antilock
  braking, electronic stabilization, automatic emergency braking, adaptive headlights, obstacle detection, and speed warnings;
- lane assistance, such as lane departure warnings, lane-keeping assistance, and blind-spot monitoring;
- backing assistance, such as rear-view cameras, backup warnings, and
  rear cross traffic warnings; and
- driver monitoring/assistance systems, such as drowsiness alert, alco-
  hol impairment detection, temperature and roadway condition warnings, safety exit assistance, and parking assistance.

Many of these systems only warn drivers of issues, which would be classi-
fied as Level 1 automation. Others actively control some portion of driver
responsibilities, such as adaptive cruise control directing the gas pedal.

Driver monitoring can be accomplished with a variety of systems. Driving
behavior such as lane keeping can be monitored. Impairment can be assessed
with a Breathalyzer. Video recognition of activities signaling driver inat-
tentiveness, such as looking at external objects, reading, applying makeup,
or dialing or texting on a hand-held device—which all increase the risk of
vehicle crashes—can also be used.

As an example of market penetration, the partial automation feature of
automatic emergency braking was not offered commercially at all prior to
model year 2008. By 2019 this feature was standard on roughly a quarter of
all models and offered as an option on an additional third of all models.

Newer partial automation systems are becoming available, offered commercially as options on premium vehicles. Examples are enhanced night
vision and obstacle identification systems. Enhanced night vision typically
uses the infrared spectrum and can penetrate through fog. Obstacle identi-

fication is used to identify pedestrians or large animals. As with other driver assistance systems, over time these options should improve in capability and reduce in cost due to scale economies.

The cost of partial automation systems depends on the amount of automation used, scale economies, and manufacturing improvements. In 2015 Toyota offered blind-spot, forward collision, and lane-departure warnings as a package of options for $600.[19] Since then, these systems have become standard on Toyota vehicles. Partial automation systems can also increase the cost of vehicle repairs since the systems need recalibration in case of damage.

While these partial automation systems can reduce the stress and fatigue of driving, their main impact will be on safety. Even with the first-generation implementations, vehicles with driver warning systems had slightly less frequent and less severe crashes, even though the repairs for the warning systems tend to increase the cost of a crash.[20] Active collision avoidance braking and improved warning systems should be even more effective. The result will be fewer injuries and fatalities with partially automated vehicles. Khan et al. (2019) estimated that the cost of equipping the entire US light duty fleet with three warning systems (forward collision warning, blind-spot monitoring, and lane-departure warning) would cost roughly $16 billion annually but would result in social safety benefits of $37 billion annually and private safety benefits of $32 billion annually. The difference in social and private benefits consist of emergency responder and incident congestion costs. Thus, safety benefits are larger than the costs of the partial automation systems themselves even for simple warning systems.

Another benefit of partial automation is improved fuel efficiency. Data from a large number of vehicle trips in Sweden demonstrate that Volvo vehicles using adaptive cruise control (ACC) had 5 to 7 percent lower fuel consumption than comparable trips without ACC.[21] Of course, ACC could be designed to be more or less fuel efficient depending on the choice of acceleration rates, but fuel economy savings are possible relative to typical driver behaviors. A policy challenge is to encourage effective versions of such software.

While partial automation is available on new vehicles, the slow turnover of the vehicle fleet means that most vehicles will not have these technologies for a decade or more. The average age of vehicles in operation is twelve years,[22] so even the required rear-view video would be on only roughly 50 percent of vehicles by 2028. Moreover, only rear-view cameras are required, so many vehicles come with very limited driver assistance safety systems.

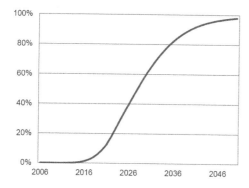

Figure 3. The percentage of vehicles expected to have automatic emergency braking over time. Data from National Academies of Science, Engineering and Medicine, "Critical Issues in Transportation 2019," and "Renewing the National Commitment to the National Interstate Highway System: A Foundation for the Future" (Washington, DC: The National Academies Press, 2018).

Some systems can be retrofitted, but there is little evidence of such investment. Even though partial automation systems are commercially available, they will not be universal for many decades. As an example, figure 3 shows the percentage of vehicles expected to have automatic emergency braking in the future. A 50 percent penetration of this feature is not expected until 2030.

A likely scenario for partial automation is continued increasing penetration into the vehicle fleet. Required systems such as rear-view video will increase the most rapidly. Market acceptance of features such as drowsiness monitoring is unknown. It is also possible that vehicles equipped with levels 4 or 5 automation may be manually driven with partial automation assistance. As a result, partial automation systems will likely be in use for many decades. It is also likely that vehicles without these driver assistance automation systems will still be in use for many decades.

A number of policy and research issues still exist for partial automation systems. Some notable examples:

- How might widespread use of adaptive cruise control affect roadway traffic flow, energy use, and air emissions?
- Should additional partial automation systems be required, or should insurance companies offer lower premiums for vehicles equipped with these systems?
- Will driver warning systems increase problems of distracted driving?
- Will price reductions in partial automation systems continue as technology improves and more vehicles are equipped with these systems?
- How can the most effective versions of variable applications, such as adaptive cruise control and lane following, be identified and encouraged?

HIGHLY AUTOMATED, DRIVERLESS VEHICLES

Media and popular attention on CAV has tended to focus on the prospects for widespread deployment of highly automated, driverless vehicles. The 2007 DARPA Urban Challenge described earlier demonstrated the feasibility of driverless vehicles in typical traffic. The commercial challenge is to make driverless vehicles robust and reliable under varied conditions and in mixed traffic.

Advances in computing and sensing technologies are crucial to achieving reliable driverless vehicle operations. Typical sensors would include

- radar mounted on the front, rear, and sides of a vehicle to measure distance to obstacles;
- video cameras mounted for 360-degree views for obstacle and lane detection and traffic sign identification;
- lidar ("light detection and ranging," using a pulsating laser) to provide more detailed detection of obstacles and roadway paths; and
- environmental sensors to identify temperature and precipitation.

In addition, in-vehicle sensors provide data on vehicle performance and situation, such as speed and direction. All of these sensors provide a huge amount of data on the vehicle and its surroundings.

Global Navigation Satellite Systems (GNSS) and stored roadway maps are a common feature for highly automated vehicles. These maps provide fine detail on lane geometry and operational rules such as stop signs. Updates are needed regularly to ensure accuracy. Real-time data on construction, maintenance, or incidents can also be used.

Multiple levels of software are required for perception, planning, and control. At the perception level, sensor data must be integrated with map information and a model of the vehicle's surroundings including identification of obstacles. Planning for vehicle actions involves both strategic decisions about routes and tactical issues of lane choice. Control of vehicle actions converts plans into specific outputs for vehicle functions such as throttle or turning.

Currently, driverless on-road vehicles are in limited use. Many localities prohibit on-road highly automated vehicles (HAVs) unless a human driver is overseeing the vehicle operations. In addition, many HAVs are limited to special conditions such as interstate highways or low-speed applications. For example, Tesla's autopilot can be used hands free in many circumstances, but drivers are directed to regularly engage. Low-speed driverless shuttles are being used in demonstration trials in a variety of designated locations such as campuses, airports, and urban areas. A few demonstration trials of ride-hailing services from transportation network companies are starting to appear. Level 5 delivery robots are also being deployed.

Remote human supervision of HAVs is another business strategy. Companies such as Phantom Auto, Starsky Robotics, and even Waymo have developed systems for automated vehicle remote control.[23] This system demonstrates the convergence on the automated vehicle technology, connected vehicle technology, and human supervision, with all three systems playing a critical role.

Commercial competition is keen among software system developers for high levels of vehicle automation. Participants include software companies (such as Aurora, Argo AI, and Waymo), traditional vehicle manufacturers (in various partnerships), transportation network companies (such as Uber), and systems suppliers (such as Continental and Intel).

There are also competing business visions for the introduction of driverless vehicles. One approach would constrain driverless vehicles to fleet operations. These fleet vehicles would be available to the public as shared vehicles or used directly by the fleet operators for tasks such as deliveries. Alternatively, driverless vehicles could be sold to private individuals in the same way that conventional vehicles are sold. These privately owned vehicles might also be used to provide transportation network company ride-hailing services. Market forces and regulation will determine which vision will prevail.

Driverless vehicles could have profound impacts on transportation systems. Since a high fraction of vehicle crashes are caused by driver errors, driverless vehicles have the potential for significantly improving roadway safety. NHTSA estimated that the total costs of vehicle crashes in the United States was $277 billion annually in 2010,[24] so highly automated vehicles, if safe and effective, would be quite valuable.

Reliability in mixed traffic and with varying conditions is a considerable challenge. For example, at 9:58 pm on Sunday, March 18, 2018, a highly automated vehicle using a system developed by Uber Technologies struck and killed a pedestrian walking a bicycle across a street in Tempe, Arizona.[25] Sensors detected an obstacle but did not identify it as a pedestrian until seconds before the crash (figure 4). Factory-installed emergency braking was disabled for the automation software. The driver was not actively engaged in controlling the vehicle until a second before collision. The overall effect from the crash and the resulting publicity has been a slowdown in HAV deployments; system testing and improvement continue.

A second area of concern for highly automated vehicles is their ability to maneuver in mixed traffic. For example, drivers and cyclists occasionally use

Figure 4. Fatal crash of a pedestrian and a highly automated vehicle. *Left*: Path of pedestrian and vehicle. *Right*: post-crash view of vehicle. Source: NTSA, 2018.

hand signals to communicate with other drivers. Similarly, police use hand signals to direct traffic when needed. Identifying and interpreting such hand gestures is a major challenge for technology. Eye contact between drivers is often used to determine whether it is safe to proceed through an uncontrolled intersection. Figure 5 is a hand-painted sign posted in Pittsburgh in 2016 to highlight a concern about HAVs in mixed traffic.

As automated technology improves and more experience is obtained, the reliability of HAVs should also improve. As of 2019, Waymo has logged over a million miles of autonomous driving with only one occurrence of software disengagement (requiring manual driver takeover) per 11,000 miles of driving.[26] This disengagement rate for Waymo has improved by at least 50 percent in recent years.

Figure 5. Hand-painted sign highlighting a concern for highly automated vehicles in mixed traffic. Photo by Chris Hendrickson.

While safety is a primary motivation for developing highly automated vehicles, other significant impacts are likely. Elderly and mobility-impaired travelers would have new options for safe travel. With a lower burden of driving, travel demand may be enhanced, especially for ride-hailing services, leading to more vehicle miles traveled. As noted earlier, driverless vehicles could be programmed to reduce energy use and emissions per mile traveled compared to manual drivers. Urban form may also be affected, especially in terms of parking requirements.

Vehicle operations could also be affected. Traffic flow stability could be improved with good programming and speed harmonization, eliminating shock waves of abrupt speed shifts. Vehicle-following gaps could be altered, improving effective lane capacity. Increases in bottleneck capacity might also be possible with automated driving for enhanced lane and speed control.

There will also be impacts on employment. Some truck driving jobs could be eliminated, reducing the perennial need for additional drivers. Other truck drivers may find their jobs changing to focus on automated vehicle supervision and customer relations. New jobs will be created for maintenance of automated systems.

A number of policy and research challenges exist for highly automated vehicles:

- How can driverless vehicles be made to become highly reliable in varying conditions?
- What programs are needed to help replaced fleet drivers transition to different roles?
- Which business models will prevail in different HAV markets?
- How can public transportation be improved as fully automated vehicles become increasingly available?
- What policies can encourage shared passenger use and discourage single- or zero-passenger trips?
- How can municipalities manage reductions in revenue from parking fees and from vehicle code violation fines?

CONNECTED VEHICLES

Connected vehicles have onboard electronic communication links. As with automation technology, there are various possible levels and types of such communications. Applications of connected vehicle technology as described below do not require any vehicle automation. When these systems identify a safety issue, they provide a warning to the driver through a visual, audible, or haptic signal. These connected vehicle systems can also provide nonsafety information to a driver to such as routing or speed control to improve vehicle efficiency.

Some autonomous vehicle systems require no connectivity to other vehicles or the infrastructure, as was demonstrated in the DARPA Urban Grand Challenge. However, connected vehicle systems can be augmented by automation, particularly when a driver may be distracted or slow to react, and automated systems can be augmented by connectivity when sensors are limited in situations such as "seeing around corners."

Most vehicles have onboard cellular communications capabilities in the form of smartphones. A variety of applications are in regular use to aid travelers. Traveler information applications can suggest the best routes to use. Telephone communication with emergency services enhances security and response to incidents such as accidents or breakdowns. Real-time bus arrival enhances service for riders. Ride-hailing companies use cellular communications to match trip demands to travel suppliers.

Cellular communications can also be used for accessing a vehicle's onboard diagnostic systems. The OnStar Corporation (a subsidiary of General Motors) provides a common system for this purpose. Other commercial vendors use the OBD-II standardized digital communications port to access the onboard diagnostics system. Preventive maintenance and emergency services can be improved with this information.

Cellular communications can also distract drivers, so not all connectivity is beneficial all the time. At the same time, travelers can benefit from having the capability of communicating with family, friends, and associates.

Smartphones can provide cellular and data services to travelers not using private vehicles, such as bikers, transit users, and pedestrians. A variety of applications are available. For example, many transit systems provide real-time information on vehicle locations to inform transit users when vehicles will be available. Route planners are useful for all these modes. Weather forecast applications are widespread.

Geographic coverage of cellular services is high but not comprehensive. Different carriers vary in their geographic coverage, and some areas are not served by the most recent 4G networks. Cellular communication can also be subject to significant congestion effects. As a result, some trucking communication systems rely on more comprehensive, dedicated satellite communications.

Connectivity with the satellite-based global positioning system (GPS) is common in US vehicles. This allows every vehicle's location to be known. Travelers can track their progress using GPS in conjunction with roadway maps. Applications can also use GPS information to track roadway congestion and roadway link speeds.

Trucking connectivity and GPS stems can monitor vehicle positions, vehicle conditions, and driver behavior to improve operations. For example, shippers can track shipment progress in real time.

In contrast to vehicle automation features, cellular connectivity and GPS use have not required the long period of fleet turnover to be accomplished. While many vehicles have built-in cellular services, most communication is accomplished through private smartphones. By 2019, 96 percent of Americans had a cellphone of some type, with 81 percent having smartphones.[27] Smartphone use has grown from only 31 percent in 2011.

Using connectivity to inform vehicle operations requires greater reliability and less latency than existing cellular networks provide. An example is connectivity for truck platooning. Acceleration and deceleration can be coordinated for multitruck platoons. Cost savings are available in the form of aerodynamic efficiencies to reduce fuel costs and possibly in the use of driverless trucks. While numerous demonstrations have shown that truck platooning is technically feasible, pairing trucks and ensuring that braking reactions are consistent provide practical challenges for widespread adoption.

Allocation of the 5.9 GHz spectrum for intelligent transportation systems[28] would enable the use of Dedicated Short-Range Communications (DSRC) with low latency and good capacity for connectivity. In 2014 the NHTSA proposed a regulation that would require DSRC in all new vehicles.[29] The organization concluded that the safety benefits of intersection movement and left-turn assist alone would justify the use of the 5.9 GHz spectrum and the cost of connectivity technology. However, at the time of this writing they have not announced a decision about proceeding with this regulation.

Effective vehicle-to-vehicle (V2V) and vehicle-to-other (V2X) connectivity could enhance safety and transportation operations. Collision possibilities with obstacles could be communicated, as is currently done with airplanes and ships. Traffic merging could be smoother with V2V communications. In the extreme, intersections could be controlled with V2V agreements rather than with traffic signals or signs.

The combination of connectivity and partial automation should provide additional safety benefits. For example, Yue et al. (2018) estimated that the combination could reduce light-duty crash rates by 33 percent and truck crash rates by 41 percent. Thus, for rather modest investments, social costs and the number of fatalities could be reduced significantly.

Connected Vehicle Evolution

At the encouragement of the Intelligent Transportation Society of America, in 1999 the Federal Communications Commission designated 75 MHz of the 5.9 GHz spectrum in 1999 for DSRC applications of Intelligent Transportation Systems in order to improve safety and decrease congestion, air pollution, and energy use.[30]

In 2012 the US DOT's Connected Vehicle Research Program of the Intelligent Transportation Systems Joint Program Office (ITS-JPO) awarded the University of Michigan Transportation Research Institute the Safety Pilot Model Deployment program. The "Safety Pilot" was a three-year program to test connected-vehicle DSRC applications with thousands of vehicles along with roadside devices on the streets of Ann Arbor, Michigan. Safety Pilot data was used to inform NHTSA's January 12, 2017, Notice of Proposed Rulemaking, announcing a proposal to mandate that newly manufactured light-duty vehicles be equipped with DSRC radios for V2V communications.[31]

Following the Safety Pilot, in 2016 the ITS-JPO awarded Connected Vehicle Pilot deployments to Wyoming, New York City, and Tampa, Florida, to further test real-world applications of vehicle-to-vehicle and vehicle-to-infrastructure technology.[32]

The aforementioned NHTSA V2V rulemaking was stalled when 5G cellular technology was presented as an alternative to DSRC. Some automakers who were originally supportive of DSRC, such as Ford, switched their support to 5G along with companies such as Qualcomm.[33]

Connected and Automated Vehicle Impacts

A variety of benefits can be obtained from the integration of connectivity and automation technology.[34] Vehicle-to-vehicle connectivity can provide:

- cooperative collision warnings and alerts for hazards such as roadway debris;
- cooperative collision mitigation or avoidance with turning maneuvers and automatic braking;
- cooperative adaptive cruise control to enable smoother, more stable traffic flow and platooning;
- automated maneuver coordination for smoother merging or conflict resolution at intersections; and
- transit bus connection protection.

.nfrastructure connectivity can provide additional benefits such as
 d traffic signal coordination, identification of bicyclists and pedestri-
 detailed traffic flow information for trip planning, and emergency services.
A number of policy and research challenges exist for vehicle connectivity.
We need to consider the following questions:

- Which technology will be used for advanced connectivity?
- How can connectivity best aid traffic movement through signalized intersections, merges, work zones, and roadway bottlenecks?
- What standards will be developed for connectivity and associated applications?
- What the time frame can be expected for implementation of advanced connectivity in the vehicle fleet?

WHAT DO WE DO NOW?

The federal government continues to be reluctant to regulate or legislate "winners and losers" in both the connected and automated vehicle industries, and states continue to provide a patchwork of legislation, regulation, and guidance. The industry has begun to collaborate on standards and outreach for public acceptance. Cities like Pittsburgh, in conjunction with the AV testing industry, have developed innovative models of voluntary compliance to navigate balance of enabling innovation and ensuring public safety.

The Pittsburgh Principles include the following:[35]

- instituting transparent lines of communication between the City and partners testing autonomous vehicles, and annual reports on the implementation of AV policies;
- promoting automated driving systems that encourage high vehicle occupancy with lower or no emissions, and lower cost and equitable transportation options;
- engaging industry leaders and community stakeholders to collaboratively facilitate the further development and deployment of self-driving technology.

The State of Pennsylvania created an Autonomous Vehicle Policy Task Force with participation from representatives of academia, industry, many state agencies, and community stakeholder groups. This resulted in an innovative approach to voluntary standards for AV testing on public roadways.

Furthermore, the states of Michigan, Ohio, and Pennsylvania have developed the Smart Belt Coalition as a multistate connected and automated

Table 1. Timeline of CAV developments

Year	Date	Selected CAV Milestone
1999	October 21	FCC allocates 75 MHz of the 5.9 GHz spectrum for intelligent transportation services
2007	November 3	DARPA Urban Grand Challenge
2011	August 31	USDOT awards Safety Pilot Model Deployment in Michigan
2012	September 25	California enacts first law for automated vehicles
2013	September 4	CMU takes public officials on 33 mile Level 4 CAV tour on public roads
	September 18	Google releases news of vehicle fleet operating 500,000 miles with its "Chauffer" system
2014	April 7	NHTSA issues final rule on requiring backup cameras
2015	September 11	Ten automakers commit to make automatic emergency braking standard
2016	May 7	First automated vehicle fatality with Tesla's autopilot in Florida
	September 1	USDOT announces NHTSA's first guidance on automated vehicles
	September 14	Uber's first autonomous public ride-hailing service debuts in Pittsburgh
2017	January 12	NHTSA issues Notice of Proposed Rulemaking to Mandate Vehicle-to-Vehicle (V2V) Communications for New Light Vehicles
	June 26	USDOT ITS-JPO awards Connected Vehicle Pilot deployments in Florida, New York, and Wyoming
2018	March 1	First pedestrian fatality from an Uber automated vehicle in Arizona
	October 4	USDOT issues Automated Vehicles 3.0: Preparing for the Future of Transportation
2019	March 1	Thirty-five states enact automated vehicle legislation, regulation, or guidance

vehicle test bed to explore CAV technology and policy challenges and to collaborate on solutions for wide-scale deployment.

The authors of this report were actively engaged in the policy examples cited above but acknowledge that municipalities, states, and countries are dealing with CAV technology through many different approaches. These various initiatives enable innovation while protecting public safety. They expose citizens to benefits of new technology and begin to address the community concerns of privacy, security, and equity. What is important is that communities embrace this new technology, learn from the successes and mistakes of other communities, and begin to coordinate their response and investments. If we look at the example of the deployment of US automobile roadways at the turn of the century, it was decades until the federally designated interstate highways and their subsequent standards were adopted.

To navigate the disruptive and rapid CAV evolution, government, industry, academia, and community organizations should continue to collaborate on standards, policies for safe testing and deployment, and transparency and forthright communications with the public.

ACKNOWLEDGMENTS

Financial support from the Urban Transportation Center at University of Illinois Chicago and Carnegie Mellon University's Traffic21 Institute and Mobility21 USDOT National University Transportation Center is gratefully acknowledged.

Notes

1. Defense Advanced Research Projects Agency, "DARPA Urban Challenge," www.darpa.mil/about-us/timeline/darpa-urban-challenge, accessed 2019.

2. Lawrence D. Burns with Christopher Shulgan, *Autonomy: The Quest to Build the Driverless Car—And How It Will Reshape Our World*. New York: Ecco Harper-Collins, 2018.

3. Carnegie Mellon University Real-Time and Multimedia Systems Lab, "Media Coverage of the Sept 04, 2013 Event," http://rtml.ece.cmu.edu/Shuster/media.html.

4. Adam Fisher, "Google's Self-Driving Cars: A Quest for Acceptance," *Popular Science*, September 18, 2013, www.popsci.com/cars/article/2013-09/google-self-driving-car.

5. Damon Lavrinc, "Autonomous Vehicle Now Legal in California," *Wired*, September 25, 2012, www.wired.com/2012/09/sb1298-signed-governor.

6. National Conference of State Legislatures, "Autonomous Vehicles | Self-Driving Vehicles Enacted Legislation," accessed March 19, 2019 (last updated February 18, 2020), www.ncsl.org/research/transportation/autonomous-vehicles-self-driving-vehicles-enacted-legislation.aspx.

7. Greg Gardner, "Feds Issue First Self-Driving Vehicle Guidelines" *Detroit Free Press*, September 19, 2016, accessed online at www.freep.com.

8. National Highway Traffic Safety Administration, "Automated Driving Systems," accessed August 18, 2019, www.nhtsa.gov/vehicle-manufacturers/automated-driving-systems.

9. Doug Newcomb, "2013: Year of the Autonomous Vehicle," *PC Magazine*, December, 26, 2013, www.pcmag.com/commentary/319174/2013-the-year-of-the-autonomous-car.

10. Alex Davies, "We Take a Ride in the Self Driving Uber Roaming Pittsburgh," *Wired*, September, 14, 2016, www.wired.com/2016/09/self-driving-autonomous-uber-pittsburgh.

11. Resse Counts, "Toyota, VW and GM Partner on Autonomous Vehicle Education," Autoblog, January 9, 2019, www.autoblog.com/2019/01/09/pave-autonomous-vehicle-education.

12. Jennifer Shuttleworth, SAE, accessed August 18, 2019 (last updated January 7, 2019), www.sae.org/news/2019/01/sae-updates-j3016-automated-driving-graphic.

13. Junko Yoshida, "UL Takes Autonomy Standards Plunge," *EE Times*, April 16, 2019, www.eetimes.com/document.asp?doc_id=1334569#.

14. Jennifer Shuttleworth, SAE, accessed August 18, 2019 (last updated January 7, 2019), www.sae.org/news/2019/01/sae-updates-j3016-automated-driving-graphic.

15. National Highway Traffic Safety Administration, 2019, "Automated Vehicles for Safety," accessed August 18, 2019, www.nhtsa.gov/technology-innovation/automated-vehicles-safety.

16. Planet Money, "Remembering When Driverless Elevators Drew Skepticism," National Public Radio, July 31, 2015, www.npr.org/2015/07/31/427990392/remembering-when-driverless-elevators-drew-skepticism.

17. National Highway Traffic Safety Administration, "Federal Motor Vehicle Safety Standards: Rear Visibility," *Federal Register*, April 7, 2014. www.federalregister.gov/documents/2014/04/07/2014-07469/federal-motor-vehicle-safety-standards-rear-visibility.

18. Jeff S. Bartlett, "Forward-Collision Warning with Braking to Become Standard," *Consumer Reports*, last updated September 11, 2015, www.consumerreports.org/cro/cars/why-forward-collision-warning-and-automatic-emergency-braking-ne.

19. Corey D. Harper, Chris T. Hendrickson, and Constantine Samaras, "Cost and Benefit Estimates of Partially-Automated Vehicle Collision Avoidance Technologies," *Accident Analysis & Prevention*, 2016, 95, 104–115.

20. Abdullah Khan, Corey D. Harper, Chris T. Hendrickson, and Constantine Samaras, "Net-Societal and Net-Private Benefits of Some Existing Vehicle Crash Avoidance Technologies," *Accident Analysis & Prevention*, 2019, 125, 207–216.

21. Lei Zhu, Jeffrey Gonder, Eric Bjarkvik, Mitra Pouabdollah, and Bjorn Lindenberg, "An Automated Vehicle Fuel Economy Benefits Evaluation Framework Using Real-World Travel and Traffic Data," *IEEE Intelligent Transportation Systems*, Fall 2019, doi: 10.1109/MITS.2019.2919537.

22. Bureau of Transportation Statistics, 2019, "Average Age of Automobiles and Light Trucks in the United State," www.bts.gov/content/average-age-automobiles-and-trucks-operation-united-states.

23. Sasha Lekach, "This Is What It's Like to Control an Autonomous Car from Miles Away," *Mashable*, June 1, 2019, https://mashable.com/article/remote-controlled-autonomous-driving-vehicles-trucks.

24. L. Blincoe, T. R. Miller, E. Zaloshnja, and B. A. Lawrence, "The Economic and Societal Impact of Motor Vehicle Crashes, 2010 Report No. DOT HS 812 013," National Highway Traffic Safety Administration, 2015. Washington, DC.

25. National Highway Traffic Safety Administration, "Automated Driving Systems," accessed August 18, 2019, www.nhtsa.gov/vehicle-manufacturers/automated-driving-systems.

26. Alan Ohnsman, "Waymo Tops Self-Driving Car 'Disengagement' Stats as GM Cruise Gains and Tesla Is AWOL," *Forbes*, February 13, 2019, www.forbes.com/sites/

alanohnsman/2019/02/13/waymo-tops-self-driving-car-disengagement-stats-as-gm
-cruise-gains-and-tesla-is-awol/#432ebf8731ec.

27. Pew Research Center, "Mobile Fact Sheet," 2019, www.pewinternet.org/fact
-sheet/mobile.

28. National Academies of Sciences, Engineering, and Medicine, *The Vital Federal
Role in Meeting the Highway Innovation Imperative* (Washington, DC: The National
Academies Press, 2019), doi: 10.17226/25511.

29. National Highway Traffic Safety Administration, 2014a, "Advanced Notice of Pro-
posed Rulemaking. Federal Motor Vehicle Safety Standards: Vehicle-to-Vehicle (V2V)
Communications," 79 FR 49270, August 20, 2019, www.regulations.gov/document
?D=NHTSA-2014-0022-0002.

30. Federal Communications Commission, "FCC Allocates Spectrum in 5.9 GHz
Range for Intelligent Transportation Systems Uses Action Will Improve the Efficiency
of the Nation's Transportation Infrastructure," October 21, 1999, https://transition.fcc
.gov/Bureaus/Engineering_Technology/News_Releases/1999/nret9006.html.

31. National Highway Traffic Safety Administration NPRM, 2017, "Federal Motor
Vehicle Safety Standards; V2V Communications" www.federalregister.gov/documents/
2017/01/12/2016-31059/federal-motor-vehicle-safety-standards-v2v-communications.

32. Intelligent Transportation System—Joint Program Office, "Connected Vehicle
Pilot Deployment Program Fact Sheet," August 18, 2019, www.its.dot.gov/factsheets/
pdf/JPO_CVPilot.pdf.

33. Gary Elinoff, "Is C-V2X Overtaking DSRC in Vehicle-to-Vehicle Communications?" *All About Circuits*, March 5, 2019, www.allaboutcircuits.com/news/is-c-v2x
-overtaking-dsrc-in-vehicle-to-vehicle-communications-platform.

34. National Academies of Science, Engineering and Medicine, "Renewing the
National Commitment to the National Interstate Highway System: A Foundation
for the Future," 2018, http://nap.edu/25334.

35. Pittsburgh, Pennsylvania, "Pittsburgh Principles for Autonomous Vehicles,"
2019, https://pittsburghpa.gov/domi/autonomous-vehicles.

Automation of Freight Systems

KAZUYA KAWAMURA

In 2016 a total of $18.1 trillion worth of freight was transported within the United States, generating 5.1 trillion ton-miles of movement across various modes.[1] Approximately 70 percent of the value and 40 percent of the ton-miles was moved by trucks. The US Department of Transportation projects that by 2045 the total value of freight shipments in the United States will reach $37 trillion, doubling the 2016 figure, and that total ton-miles will increase by more than 50 percent.[2] What is most concerning is that the growth in truck ton-miles is expected to exceed 62 percent for the same time period. To put this in perspective, it is worthwhile to relate it to projected population changes. According to Census Bureau estimates, the US population is expected to increase by only 20 percent between 2016 and 2045,[3] which means that the average amount of freight movement per person would rise dramatically. The rate of ton-miles per person for freight moved (other than by pipelines) was approximately 12,500 in 2016. By 2045, if those estimates are correct, the rate of ton-miles per person will be about 20,000—a 57 percent increase. In other words, Americans are expected to be considerably more "freight intensive" in the coming decades, continuing the recent general trend of supply-chain globalization. Given this backdrop, it is interesting that automation of freight systems has attracted relatively modest attention from the public and the media compared to automation for passenger cars. Part of the reason is the fragmented nature of the freight transportation sector; in addition, the wariness of the industry, which understands the complexity and unpredictability of technology adoption from having seen a number of "next big things" come and go in the past, might also play a role.[4] Yet automation has already taken place in a major way at one of the key components of the global freight system: maritime container ports. This chapter uses lessons learned from that experience to elucidate automation in other parts of the freight systems.

The goal of this chapter is to provide a high-level insight on how automation technologies can be deployed in the freight sector during the next decade or so, and how that may impact urban areas. The next section introduces paradigms of freight transportation that are relevant when considering the adoption and effect of automation. Subsequent sections discuss trends of automation in various components of freight systems. The final section provides a summary with some thoughts on the implication for urban areas.

FREIGHT TRANSPORTATION AND TECHNOLOGY ADOPTION

Freight System Components

To understand technology adoption in freight transportation, it is important to take an end-to-end systems perspective. Movement of freight can cover thousands of miles, changing modes and often going through multiple stages of consolidation and deconsolidation, making it fundamentally distinct from passenger transportation, which typically moves a single unit—a person—from an origin to a destination. Figure 1 shows a simple example of imported retail goods that come in from a port and are delivered to stores located in an urban area in another part of the country. Ports, distribution centers (DCs), and retail stores are "nodes" where freight may change vehicles or transportation modes or may go through consolidation or deconsolidation. In some cases, value-adding operations such as light manufacturing or finishing of products can take place at nodes. In reality, shipments may go through more or fewer DCs along the way, depending on how a particular supply chain system is configured. As a general rule, however, shippers and carriers strive to minimize "handling" of goods to minimize the cost and, most importantly, the risk of damage. Some commodities, such as gravel, may move only within a relatively limited area because it does not make economic sense to move heavy and cheap goods over long distances.

Due to the multidimensional characteristics of freight systems, the freight transportation sector's heterogeneity far exceeds that of passenger transportation, complicating efforts to understand how automation will occur and what it will mean. In terms of adopting automation technologies, there are clear differences in functions required by the components shown in the figure—the port area, the line haul, and urban freight—and thus automation is likely to take different paths and roll out on different schedules.

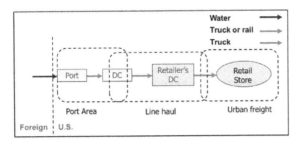

Figure 1. Simplified example of freight flow for imported retail products. Drawn by the author.

Automation technologies for moving freight between nodes (e.g., from a port to a distribution center) are different from those used for operations within nodes (e.g., at a warehouse, a port, etc.). Since it is much easier to create a controlled environment for the latter, automation is further ahead at the nodes than in the "links" that connect the nodes. In fact, while most warehouses today incorporate some level of automation, and some can even operate without human operators, the movement of trucks and trains is still dependent on humans (although assistance from information technologies is common). Automation at the nodes typically uses some form of autonomous (and in some cases connected) vehicles. The most common and mature of these are the Automated Guided Vehicles (AGVs) that are used at factories, warehouses, ports, and elsewhere—nearly anywhere that provides a controlled environment with limited access. Automated Lift Vehicles (ALVs) add the function of picking up and dropping off cargo. While AGVs need to work in tandem with cranes or forklifts, an ALV can move cargo within a node on its own, drastically increasing the flexibility of operation. Modern automated ports and warehouses often use both AGVs and ALVs. While AGVs and ALVs in use today typically rely on some type of markers or transponders embedded in the floor or in vertical walls for navigation, the next generation will use technologies such as LiDAR (Light Detection and Ranging) Sensors or cameras, which allow AGVs to be more flexible in terms of applicable environment.

In addition to functional and environmental distinctions, different supply chains and logistics system configurations required to efficiently produce and move various commodities further exacerbate the heterogeneity of freight transportation. For example, transportation of bulk commodities such as grain would not be the same as the system shown in figure 1, and the operations that take place within the nodes would be vastly different from those for containerized goods such as retail products. Yet another layer of the freight sector's heterogeneity is shipment type. Temperature-controlled shipments required for certain types of goods can be extremely expensive. Expedited shipments (e.g., same-day or next-day deliveries) are another example. These customized shipments are extremely expensive because separate logistics systems must be used to distribute them. For example, a study found that for a pharmaceutical company, the average transportation cost of refrigerated shipments is fifty times greater than that for ambient shipments.[5] The same study found that "next-day AM" deliveries are two to five times more costly than regular "next-day" shipments. As these examples illustrate, freight and logistics industries are highly complex and segmented, each with its own characteristics, needs, and opportunities. As such, the development and deployment of automation technologies will take different forms and paths for different segments of the overall industry.

It is widely recognized among freight transportation professionals that urban freight, or "last mile," is where the most urgent need exists for technological innovation, as business to consumer (B2C) shipments are increasing at an explosive rate, driven by the growth of e-commerce. E-commerce sales in the United States have been growing at an annual rate of around 15 percent or more since 2010[6] and are expected to maintain a similar rate of growth for the foreseeable future.

The line-haul portion typically accounts for the largest *share* of the end-to-end cost of domestic transportation, but in terms of marginal cost per mile, the line-haul is the most efficient.[7] On the other hand, urban freight is the least efficient. The "last mile" can account for 50 percent or more of the total logistics cost for a good even if it travels thousands of miles. Figure 2 shows a breakdown of the marginal cost of truck operation, according to a

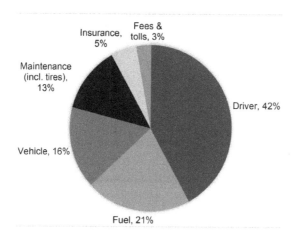

Figure 2. Share of the average marginal cost per mile of a motor carrier, 2016. Based on data from Alan Hooper and Dan Murray, "An Analysis of the Operational Costs of Trucking" (American Transportation Research Institute, 2017), 23.

survey by the American Transportation Research Institute (ATRI). As the figure shows, drivers are the biggest cost component of running a truck. When this detail is combined with the chronic shortage of drivers in the United States, platooning and/or driverless trucks would seem to be appealing for the industry. While the percentages shown in figure 2 mostly represent tractor-trailers, the share of driver cost for straight-trucks, which are often used for urban freight operations, decreases to 32 percent while the share for maintenance and repair increases to 22 percent, presumably due to more challenging driving conditions in cities.

Freight Industry Behavior

One of the important behavioral differences between freight and passenger transportation is that the former is driven purely by competition while travel decisions for individuals are thought to be made based on a mix of rational and psychological factors. While it is believed that people typically try to limit total time spent on travel to around two and a half hours per day, as long as such a limit (called "travel time budget") is not exceeded, they are relatively unconcerned about reducing travel time further or minimizing time for each trip they take. Such "satisficing" behavior does not apply to freight transportation. For instance, in parcel delivery or interstate rail, where competition among a few firms has been going on for many decades, each firm strives to squeeze out the maximum performance from the system by minimizing cost while maximizing customer satisfaction. Firms normally use a benchmark that is based on industry norms and the performance of competitors to assess their own competitiveness, and the benchmark is constantly being updated to reflect changes in the competitive landscape. As such, there is no intrinsic level of system performance that is sufficient, so innovation and refinement are continuous processes.

On the other hand, freight businesses such as truck operators and railroads have typically been rather cautious when it comes to adopting new technologies. It is not unusual for a new technology to take decades to reach broad dissemination. For example, intermodal containers were invented in 1956, yet they truly started their explosive growth in the 1980s (and it still continues today). Automated gantry cranes used for moving containers at ports were first implemented in 1993 but became widely used only within the last several years. This can be explained by the fact that technology adoption in the freight sector is often dictated by the competitive landscape (e.g., the appearance of a first mover or adoption by a major competitor) rather than by technical feasibility. In other words, even when it becomes technically feasible, a new type of automation tends not to be adopted widely unless it is clearly proven through the real-world applications that it would bring competitive advantages and make a positive return on investment (and thus threaten the competitiveness of nonadopters).[8] As such, the timing and pace of automation are hard to predict. This is in stark contrast to the belief in "first mover advantage" that drives the technology sector, which is spearheading the wave of automation.

STATE OF AUTOMATION

Automation of supply-chain and logistics systems is not as transparent as automation of passenger transportation because much of the automation to those systems occurs in locations that are not visible to the public. However, a comparison of current states of technology adoption for three major components of freight systems, based on publicly available information, suggests that maritime ports and other nodes are the front-runners in automation.

Automation at Nodes

In 1993 the first automated gantry cranes were deployed at the port of Rotterdam in the Netherlands. While Rotterdam's automated terminal remained a novelty for a while, the technology took on added importance when the widening of the Panama Canal was approved by national referendum in 2006. The prospect of a wider Panama Canal introduced an era of supersized containerships, with capacities upward of 15,000 TEU (twenty-foot equivalent unit) that dwarfed the original Panamax-sized ships, which were able to carry only around 5,000 TEUs of cargo. Maritime ports around the world came under pressure to upgrade their container terminals to accommodate "new-Panamax" and "post-Panamax" ships. For the ports that lacked space to expand, automation was a logical solution.

Today, there are around twenty fully automated container terminals in the world, and there are many more partially automated terminals.[9] The world's largest automated container terminal is the Yangshan Deep-Water Port in Shanghai, which opened in December 2017 and can handle over 6 million TEUs annually. In the United States, two of the largest maritime container terminals in the country, Pier 400 at the Port of Los Angeles and the Middle Harbor terminal at the Port of Long Beach, are currently going through the process of automation. When completed, the automation of the Middle Harbor terminal will more than double the existing annual capacity, from 1.3 million TEUs to 3.3 million TEUs.[10] It should be noted that some automated terminals have a lower capacity than a nonautomated terminal when measured in per-hour basis because automated equipment tends to move at a slower pace. For example, the hourly capacity of the automated Middle Harbor terminal is expected to be around 70 percent of the existing level. The increase in annual capacity is achieved through the automated terminal's ability to operate around the clock. Safety is expected to improve significantly with automation as well.

Two observations can be made about automation from the experiences of ports. First is the initial cost of automation and the difficulty of generating a positive return on investment. The automation at the Port of Long Beach is expected to cost $1.3 billion to $1.5 billion. The automation of the Victoria terminal at the Port of Melbourne, which is considerably smaller than the ports in California or Shanghai, cost $400 million. According to an industry report, port automation projects around the globe have not consistently resulted in productivity increases despite the steep price tag. Surprisingly, the average change in port productivity after automation has been negative (−11 percent) according to a survey of forty port executives from around the world.[11] Automation typically improved the safety and reliability of port operation but, due to a lack of trained personnel, integration problems with external systems, and vulnerability to unexpected events, failed to produce sufficient gains in productivity to justify the investment.[12] Despite these challenges, why is a wave of automation sweeping across ports around the globe? The reason is the enormous potential of broader adoption of automation and coordination within and outside ports, which would result in a giant leap in productivity not only in the logistics and transportation industries but also in manufacturing and other business activities that rely on the global supply-chain network.

The second observation, which is derived from the point above, is the need for end-to-end deployment of automation. When automated components are not properly integrated into an end-to-end system, bottlenecks will simply shift from the automated components to downstream without improving overall efficiency. An industry publication that has raised concerns regarding "shifting bottlenecks" has stated, "Automated container terminals can help European hubs handle mega-ships and the exchanges of up to 10,000 TEU that can accompany each port call, but those efficiencies are often lost as inland-bound cargo moves from the quay to the intermodal connections."[13]

Due to the highly segmented nature of the freight sector, automation of the entire system will be slow and may never happen. Also, for some commodities, automation may be too difficult or the benefits will not be sufficient to justify it. As such, it is reasonable to expect that the first cases of system-wide logistics automation will be found in those systems that are managed by a single entity or a well-coordinated consortium (e.g., auto manufacturers or beverage producers). For other systems, automation will likely proceed gradually, at least until sufficient information on automation and integration has been collected from the first movers so that the return on investment becomes easier to estimate.

Line-Haul Components

For the line-haul portion of the freight system, which will be put under pressure to handle the increased throughput from automated container ports, vehicle technologies will be the main field of innovation. In the US market, Level 2 trucks, including Class 8 tractor-trailers, are already available.[14] Level 2 trucks, equipped with automated longitudinal and lateral movement controls, are expected to reduce accidents. While many major vehicle manufacturers are actively engaged in the development of Level 4 or 5 automation of trucks, broad deployment on public roads is most likely a decade or more away even under the best-case scenario. Aside from vehicle-based technologies, legal and infrastructure issues must be resolved before driverless vehicles can be used on public roads.[15] However, the chronic shortage of truck drivers in the United States and other developed countries will provide a strong incentive for developing and deploying automation technologies that reduce or eliminate the need for drivers. Meanwhile, the most significant impact of truck automation will likely be its effect on the ongoing effort to examine rules concerning the truck driver hours of service (HOS) regulation. The number of hours that a driver can operate a truck and also the amount of rest required between shifts are set by the rules issued by the Federal Motor Carrier Safety Administration (FMCSA). The trucking industry has long criticized the HOS regulations as too onerous and overly strict. In May 2019 the FMCSA published an advance notice of proposed rulemaking (ANPRM) concerning automated trucks.[16] While the announcement states that this effort will focus on Level 4 and 5 trucks,[17] it will likely open the avenue to reexamine the HOS rules for lesser levels of automation, especially Level 2, which is already available. In fact, dozens of comments submitted to the FMCSA since the publication of the ANPRM refer to the regulations for Level 2 automated trucks.[18]

Another technology that involves automation of trucks is platooning,[19] in which two or more trucks are connected digitally to allow the distance between them to be as little as a few feet.[20] Platooning will reduce two of the largest cost components for truck operation—fuel and driver. Although the exact amount of fuel savings depends on factors such as platoon size, road terrain, wind direction, ambient temperature, vehicle type, amount of lateral offset between the vehicles, and other factors, most studies expect that the benefit will be modest, providing no more than a 15 percent reduction using currently available technologies.[21] While even a 10 percent reduction in fuel use, which seems to be the current industry expectation with available technologies, will still have a huge impact since long-haul trucks account for about 10 percent of US petroleum use, the effort required to operate and manage platoons of trucks casts doubt on widespread adoption even if the technology is available and affordable.

Urban Freight

Arguably, urban freight is the most segmented portion of the freight transportation system. In a typical city, thousands of businesses make deliveries to customers that include other businesses (B2B) as well as individual consumers. While the most visible players in urban freight are parcel delivery companies such as UPS and FedEx, an overwhelming majority of urban freight shipments are moved by smaller businesses that serve the needs of other businesses such as hotels, schools, law offices, and construction sites.[22]

Compared with the effort to develop driverless long-distance trucks for line-haul, the automation of vehicles used for local deliveries is an understudied area. While Level 1 and 2 automation technologies will undoubtedly be used for local delivery vehicles in the near future, driverless technologies, or Levels 4 and 5 automation, for trucks in urban environments have seldom been discussed.[23] It is technologically difficult to create physical separation between freight vehicles and other vehicles, bicyclists, and pedestrians in an urban environment. A prime example is the competition for parking space in central business districts. In addition, as Gittleman and Monaco have noted,[24] drivers of local delivery vehicles perform numerous other functions, such as loading and unloading, that often take place curbside, where implementing automation equipment will be challenging. Despite such challenges, because the "last mile" is the least efficient component of freight systems, some notable progress can be made. Yamato Transport, a major parcel delivery company in Japan, has successfully tested Level 3 and 4 delivery vans on public roads. These vans are equipped with lockers that are used to hold mail, packages, and deliveries from stores and restaurants. In this system, receivers of shipments are responsible for picking up the deliveries from the vehicle's locker using a code sent via mobile phone, effectively taking care of the "last 50 feet" of shipments, a segment that is a considerable challenge for driverless vehicles. Using real-time congestion information and a route guidance system, they were able to offer receivers a choice of ten-minute windows for each delivery. During the one-year experiment in a suburb of Tokyo, they were able to achieve a missed delivery rate of 0.5 percent, which is drastically less than the 50 percent rate typical for regular delivery services.

Outside of Yamato's efforts, the most promising avenues of automation are in small robotic vehicles or drones that can deliver small packages, such as food, over a relatively short distance—a radius of three to four miles with current technology. Drones and small robotic vehicles do not travel on public roads with other vehicles, allowing them to control their own speed of operation in a relatively safe environment, making full automation easier to achieve. There are already numerous examples of such technologies being used in the United States and around the world.[25]

Many other innovations in urban freight can be combined with these automation technologies to produce synergistic impacts. Such innovations include crowd-shipping, omni-channel retail logistics, and 3D printing. In an ideal world, the end product will be urban freight systems that cross channels (B2B, B2C, C2B, inbound/outbound, etc.) and modes (trucks, crowd-shipping, nonmotorized, delivery boxes, etc.) to deliver goods cheaply and accurately on demand. At this point, however, too many uncertainties—technical, economic, and social—exist for each, making it impossible to speculate about the collective effects in the long run.

CONCLUSION

For each component of freight systems considerable efforts to increase automation are underway, albeit with different degrees of success and maturity. It is reasonable to expect that automation of container ports will continue and will result in a significant increase in the flow of goods throughout the system. Regardless of the progress made on the development of Level 4 and 5 automation for long-distance trucks, the capacity of the line-haul component, be it rail or truck, must increase to keep up with port automation. Similarly, logistics facilities where shipments are transferred, consolidated, deconsolidated, stored, and modified must evolve. The locational advantages of the sites along major freight corridors such as interstate highways and railroad main lines will be even greater than they are now. We will probably see large, technologically advanced logistics facilities pop up near interstates, ports, and airports. The Mobility Innovation Zone in Hillwood, Texas, announced in 2019,[26] fits that bill perfectly. I believe that in the United States, truck platooning will be enticing for long-distance truck operators because of the savings associated with fuel and driver cost and because it can address the chronic issue of driver shortages. Currently, there may not be sufficient opportunities to deploy platooning since the shipments on platooned vehicles must have the same origins and destinations to eliminate the need for coupling and decoupling trucks en route. However, the emergence of supersized logistics centers may increase such opportunities.

Because of the perceived benefits associated with the end-to-end automation, there will be considerable incentive to automate downstream elements that handle container traffic. It is not clear, though, if return on investment can justify the massive financial commitment required to upgrade each of those facilities. It is important to note that with the exception of very large manufacturers and retailers, no single actor has the information to assess the financial validity of end-to-end automation. More likely, investment calculations made by individual actors will not persuade them to pursue automation at the individual facility level even when such improvements would address the system-wide need. In other words, there may be a positive externality problem associated with the automation of freight systems. To this end, I believe that research is needed to quantify the system-wide benefit of automation so as to inform decision makers about the need for public intervention and support to encourage automation.

Of course, the negative effects of job losses and other changes associated with automation can outweigh the efficiency gains. The long-term decline in the cost of transportation has been a major contributing factor in many of the changes the US economic landscape has undergone in the last several decades. For example, offshoring that contributed to the shift away from manufacturing in this country was made possible by cheap transportation. Practices such as "just in time" shipments have contributed to an increase in truck trips. Cheap transportation enabled packaging designs that were driven by occupying as much shelf space as possible. Recent increases in transportation cost have prompted businesses to question those practices, however. For example, to reduce transportation costs, US firms are increasingly looking to "nearshoring"—bringing manufacturing closer—instead of offshoring. Also, packaging is increasingly driven by ease of shipping and handling as opposed to consumer appeal. The lean-supply-chain model represented by "just in time" deliveries is being rolled back to increase stocking and shipment consolidation.[27] From a societal point of view, many of these developments are beneficial. Automation of freight transportation systems would drastically lower the costs and may reverse these recent trends. These examples underscore the fact that impacts of automation will be broad, complex, and difficult to predict.

These are reasonable but also familiar predictions. Essentially, what we expect from the automation of freight systems is a continuation of the logistics evolution that has already led to tremendous improvements in the flexibility, efficiency, and speed of freight movements. The difference is that some facilities will have drastically reduced need to access labor markets, possibly exacerbating suburbanization or exurbanization.

In urban areas, however, the spatial distribution of logistics facilities should still largely depend on the distribution of population and businesses because the last mile will still be the least efficient component, and it makes sense to minimize the distance that must be covered by such a costly operation. This linkage between the spatial distributions of population and businesses and logistics facilities is where the automation of passenger vehicles and broader urban innovations would interact, much like the suburbanization of population and "logistics sprawl" that have been going on for the past few decades.[28] It is not clear what kind of impacts automated vehicles will have on patterns of consumption and residential and work location choices. But it is nearly certain that the significant reductions automation could bring to the overall cost of passenger travel—cost of time typically accounting for around 80 percent of it—will further exacerbate suburbanization. If driverless vehicles or even Level 2 or 3 automation affect the spatial distribution of houses and businesses, logistics facilities will respond to such changes. Impacts of logistics sprawl are not well understood, however. As my research has found, from the policy point of view, it is not clear what logistics sprawl means in terms of the amount of truck traffic and carbon emissions in urban areas.[29]

In terms of actual delivery of freight, the introduction of driverless passenger vehicles may reduce the burden of the last mile: such vehicles could be sent by the owners to pick up goods at distribution centers, warehouses, or other designated pickup points while the owners engage in other activities. Pickup points will need to be capable of storing, loading, and unloading shipments so that passenger vehicles can pick up goods that have been deposited by delivery trucks (manned or unmanned). If the technology to transfer goods between a delivery truck and a driverless passenger vehicle becomes available, it will present a tremendous potential to reduce freight-related traffic because passenger vehicles will be able to meet a truck along the delivery route to pick up shipments. The operating cost of driverless vehicles will be a critical factor; if it is more expensive to pick up goods than to get them delivered by trucks, owners will opt to have shipments delivered as they do today. If driverless delivery trucks are introduced ahead of driverless passenger cars, they can still offer services (like the one being tested by Yamato) to considerably improve efficiency and the customer experience with last-mile delivery.

Finally, I would like to point out that in the past, the development and deployment of urban freight automation technologies have been carried out by the private sector without significant interface or coordination with the public sector. But municipalities (and, to a degree, counties and states) are directly responsible for the environment where these machines will operate. For urban freight in particular, many of the obstacles to automation result from design or regulatory elements set by municipalities. For example, municipal codes for delivery docks, sidewalk design, loading zone management, and parking spaces can be modified to make it easier for robotic vehicles or drones to operate. As Level 4 and 5 passenger vehicles start to roam city streets, municipalities must come up with strategies to retrofit the urban built environment to accommodate the tremendous potential offered by those technologies. Historically, the freight industry has been reluctant or unable to participate in discussions that take place during such processes, missing valuable opportunities to provide input. Universities, along with Metropolitan Planning Organizations and nongovernmental organizations, can play an important role to ensure that the freight sector will be at the table when the time comes.

Notes

1. Long Nguyen and Demi Riley, "Pocket Guide to Transportation 2019," Bureau of Transportation Statistics, 2019.

2. Nguyen and Riley, "Pocket Guide."

3. Sandra L. Colby and Jennifer M. Ortman, "Projections of the Size and Composition of the US Population: 2014 to 2060: Population Estimates and Projections," US Census Bureau, 2017.

4. More recent examples include radio-frequency identification (RFID) and positive train control of railcars.

5. Knut Alicke and Martin Lösch, "Lean and Mean: How Does Your Supply Chain Shape Up?," McKinsey & Company, 2010.

6. US Census Bureau, "Quarterly Retail E-Commerce Sales 3rd Quarter 2019," *Census Bureau News*, November 19, 2019; US Census Bureau, "US E-Commerce Sales: 1999–2019," *Marketplace Pulse*, www.marketplacepulse.com/stats/us-ecommerce/us-e-commerce-sales-22.

7. Alan Hooper and Dan Murray, "An Analysis of the Operational Costs of Trucking," American Transportation Research Institute, 2017.

8. Creating and proving value is one of the factors that has slowed down the adoption of RFID. Samuel F. Wamba and Akemi T. Chatfield, "A Contingency Model for Creating Value from RFID Supply Chain Network Projects in Logistics and Manufacturing Environments," *European Journal of Information Systems* 18, no. 6 (2009): 615–36.

9. Chu Fox, Sven Gailus, Lisa Liu, and Liumin Ni, "The Future of Automated Ports," McKinsey & Company, 2018.

10. P2S Inc., Port of Long Beach, Middle Harbor Redevelopment Project, 2010.

11. P2S Inc., Port of Long Beach.

12. P2S Inc., Port of Long Beach.

13. Greg Knowler, "European Shippers: Terminal Automation Gains Lost on Inland Moves," *Journal of Commerce*, May 4, 2018.

14. Andrea Corsco and Paige Kean, "Daimler Trucks North America Introduces First SAE Level 2 Automated Truck in North America with the Freightliner New Cascadia," Daimler, January 7, 2019, https://media.daimler.com/marsMediaSite/ko/en/42189104.

15. Jason Wagner, "Revolutionizing Our Roadways: Policy Considerations for Automated Vehicle Testing in Texas," Texas A&M Transportation Institute, 2015.

16. Federal Register, "Safe Integration of Automated Driving Systems-Equipped Commercial Motor Vehicles," *Daily Journal of the United States Government*, May 28, 2019: 24,449–59.

17. Paul Lewis, "FMCSA Takes First Step in Regulating Automated Driving for Trucks and Buses," Eno Center for Transportation, *Eno Transportation Weekly*, June 3, 2019.

18. Federal Register, "Automated Driving Systems (ADS) for Commercial Motor Vehicles (CMVs); Request for Comments Concerning Federal Motor Carrier Safety Regulations (FMCSRs) Which May Be a Barrier to the Safe Testing and Deployment of ADS-Equipped CMVs on Public Roads," *Daily Journal of the United States Government*, Public Comments, March 2018–October 2019 www.regulations.gov/docketBrowser?rpp=50&so=DESC&sb=postedDate&po=0&s=%22Level%2B2%22&dct=PS&D=FMCSA-2018-0037.

19. Also called Cooperative Adaptive Cruise Control.

20. Most of the current and past testing of platooning use 30 to 50 feet of separation between trucks.

21. Auburn University, American Transportation Research Institute, Meritor WABCO, Peloton Technology, and Peterbilt Trucks, "Heavy Truck Cooperative Adaptive Cruise-Control: Evaluation, Testing, and Stakeholder Engagement for Near Term Deployment: Phase Two Final Report" (Federal Highway Administration, 2017); Beverly Kuhn, Mike Lukuc, Mohammed Poorsartep, Jason Wagner, Kevin N. Balke, Dan Middleton, Praprut Songchitruksa, Nick Wood, and Maarit Moran, "Commercial

Truck Platooning Demonstration in Texas–Level 2 Automation," Texas A&M Transportation Institute, 2017; Sadayuki Tsugawa, Sabina Jeschke, and Steven E. Shladover, "A Review of Truck Platooning Projects for Energy Savings," *IEEE Transactions on Intelligent Vehicles* 1, no. 1, 2016: 68–77.

22. In any city, the largest share of truck trips is for transporting construction material such as gravel and equipment.

23. Maury Gittleman and Kristen Monaco, "Automation Isn't About to Make Truckers Obsolete," *Harvard Business Review*, September 18, 2019.

24. Gittleman and Monaco, "Automation."

25. Charlotte Jee, "The World's First Robot Delivery Service Is Launching in the UK," *MIT Technology Review*, November 1, 2018; UW University Housing, "University Housing Launches New Starship Robot Delivery Service," University of Wisconsin–Madison (2019), November 4, 2019, www.housing.wisc.edu/2019/11/robot-delivery; Kat Lonsdorf, "Hungry? Call Your Neighborhood Delivery Robot," *Morning Edition*, March 23, 2017, National Public Radio; Andrew Hawkins, "Thousands of Autonomous Delivery Robots Are About to Descend on US College Campuses," *The Verge*, August 20, 2019, www.theverge.com/2019/8/20/20812184/starship-delivery-robot -expansion-college-campus; James Vincent, and Chaim Gartenberg, "Here's Amazon's New Transforming Prime Air Delivery Drone," *The Verge*, June 5, 2019, www .theverge.com/2019/6/5/18654044/amazon-prime-air-delivery-drone-new-design -safety-transforming-flight-video; David Schaper, "Drone Delivery Is One Step Closer to Reality," *Morning Edition*, October 18, 2019, National Public Radio.

26. Melissa Repko, "Hillwood Wants to Turn Alliancetexas into 'Mobility Innovation Zone' for Drones, Autonomous Vehicles," *Dallas Morning News*, June 30, 2019.

27. Dawn Russell, John J. Coyle, Kusumal Ruamsook, and Evelyn A. Thomchick, "The Real Impact of High Transportation Costs," *Supply Chain Quarterly*, Quarter 1, 2014.

28. Takanori Sakai, Kazuya Kawamura, and Tetsuro Hyodo, "Spatial Reorganization of Urban Logistics System and Its Impacts: Case of Tokyo," *Journal of Transport Geography* 60 (2017): 110–18.

29. Takanori Sakai, Kazuya Kawamura, and Tetsuro Hyodo, "Evaluation of the Spatial Pattern of Logistics Facilities Using Urban Logistics Land-Use and Traffic Simulator," *Journal of Transport Geography* 74 (2019): 145–60.

PART THREE

SYNOPSIS

Back to the Future

Discussing Our New Autonomous Reality

TAYLOR LONG

Autonomous vehicles (AVs) are increasingly becoming a part of our modern reality. With new pilot programs popping up all over the globe and modern vehicles becoming more autonomous each day, transportation experts and policymakers face the daunting task of planning cities that not only accommodate this new technology but also keep it in check. Like most innovations that have come before, AVs have the potential to drastically improve quality of life. Experts anticipate that they could improve roadway safety, reduce traffic congestion, create thousands of new jobs, improve work/life balance, and make spaces more accessible to people with disabilities.

While this utopian vision is filled with promise, unless they are thoughtfully and carefully introduced, AVs also have the potential to exacerbate many of the challenges cities grapple with today. Safety regulations need to ensure that these vehicles meet basic performance standards in order to function safely and effectively. Environmentalists are concerned about the carbon footprint these vehicles may have without the infrastructure and legislation needed to incentivize the manufacture of electric vehicles. While many jobs stand to be created by AVs, others will likely be displaced if workers are not adequately trained to take advantage of a changing market. Autonomous vehicles will create large swaths of data, prompting privacy and security concerns for companies, governments, and citizens. And just as AVs might improve our quality of life, some have raised concerns that they will lead to longer work days and more isolated communities rather than the other way around. Being intentional in planning for these new developments will require the cooperation of experts across institutions, sectors, and industries.

The 2019 Urban Forum provided one platform for experts in the field to discuss this emerging technology. The following paper provides a summary and synthesis of this exciting conversation spanning a variety of topics including safety, employment, big data, government regulation, and lifestyle.

SAFETY FIRST?

Many of those familiar with AVs are excited about the technology's potential to cut down on traffic accidents and improve overall safety on the road. According to Finch Fulton, Deputy Assistant Secretary for Transportation Policy at the US Department of Transportation (USDOT), there are roughly 37,000 fatalities on American roadways each year, and the majority of those accidents are caused by human error. For many AV developers and public officials alike, self-driving cars are an opportunity to eliminate accidents caused by drunk driving, speeding, or driver fatigue. But while many in the industry seem to be convinced of AV safety, the public has been slow to trust AVs. A 2019 poll conducted by Reuters/Ipsos found that more than half of Americans don't trust self-driving vehicles.[1] Drivers are hesitant to relinquish control to a robot. Experts in the field thus have a two-pronged challenge in front of them: to ensure the safety of AVs and to gain the trust of a skeptical public.

Ensuring the safety of AVs has proven to be a massive undertaking. Fulton has been among those leading the charge to determine USDOT safety standards for AVs. While the federal government has very little authority to regulate vehicles, it is responsible for setting standards for new vehicles before they get on the road, making the federal government the first line of defense in ensuring the safety of AVs. A short history lesson is useful here. The USDOT was established in 1966 by President Lyndon B. Johnson, and under USDOT the National Highway Traffic Safety Administration was created in 1970 by the Highway Safety Act. The NHTSA was intended to increase highway safety by setting and enforcing safety standards for vehicles, performing crash tests, and using their findings to set standards for vehicle manufacturers, such as seatbelt and airbag regulations.[2] This evolution of vehicle regulations has led to a set of prescriptive safety standards—regulations that mandate the number of seatbelts in a vehicle or how many inches a seat can be from the steering wheel, for example.

Since AVs may make steering wheels and other features currently in cars a thing of the past, standards need to be updated to assess the performance of vehicles rather than dictating their structure or components. This is an important next step before AVs can be allowed on the road. At USDOT, their cursory performance standards are as follows: (1) the vehicle has to be able to get from point a to point b; (2) the vehicle must keep passengers safe; (3) the vehicle must not hit people or things on the road; and (4) it must follow all local and state laws. Although these standards sound relatively straightforward, nobody seems to agree on how to achieve them, much less how to guarantee them. Some experts go so far as to say that the safety of the machine-learning algorithms AVs rely on is impossible to prove.[3] It's a problem USDOT has recently shelled out $60 million in state grants to help solve. USDOT hopes that the eight different state-level projects awarded grant money may be able to help them learn how to test the functional safety of AVs. In the meantime, the department is taking a bottom-up approach by partnering with AV developers that are willing to undergo voluntary testing. Joe Buckner, Director of Product Engineering for an AV component company called Autonomous Stuff, said he is primarily motivated by the potential safety benefits of AVs and is among those working hard to prove the safety of their products. But even though many researchers have estimated that AVs will reduce vehicular crashes by nearly 90 percent,[4] the general public has largely remained unconvinced.

In a 2017 MIT study assessing public opinion about self-driving cars, one participant said, "I don't trust technology to the point of putting my life in its hands."[5] Speakers and panelists interested in advancing AV discussed the implications of this lack of trust and how it might affect AV implementation down the road. Fulton believes that part of the issue is that people don't actually understand the technology, which is why he and other public-sector panelists are beginning to think about how to prepare the public for a driverless future. Fulton believes that a communication strategy will be a crucial part of ensuring the smooth implementation of this new technology. Without a strategy in place for educating and informing the public, technology suffers, Fulton said, citing failed experiments with supersonic airlines in Kansas City as an example. Without buy-in from the local community, cities and developers alike will have a hard time introducing these technologies when they are ready. In many ways, the airline industry offers a useful parallel. The public generally tends to be more critical of those things they cannot control and hold them to stricter standards—it's not just "people being people."

It's impossible to talk about the safety of AVs without bringing up Elaine Herzberg, the first pedestrian killed by an AV. The outcry after her death in 2018 led Uber to quickly suspend its test programs in Arizona, Pittsburgh, San Francisco, and Toronto.[6] But while Herzberg's death served as a reminder to many about the experimental nature of fully autonomous AV, the distracted nature of the test driver behind the wheel was a reminder of how easy it is to become complacent behind the wheel of a car that is running on autopilot. While research shows that most Americans aren't comfortable with fully autonomous vehicles, many said they are comfortable with semiautonomous features. According to Buckner, these semiautonomous vehicles, also called Level 3 automation, often pose a greater threat because although they don't have fully autonomous capabilities, it's easy for drivers to get too comfortable behind the wheel. Even when the driver is paying attention, Fulton said, current data shows that it takes six seconds for a test driver to react and course-correct in the case of an unexpected emergency on the road.[7] With autonomous technology where it is today, experts agree that this reaction time probably isn't quick enough.

NOW HIRING: AUTONOMOUS VEHICLE FIELD TECHNICIAN

Automation is a scary word for industrial workers. The very mention of automation conjures up images of mass layoffs and economic hardship, and the negative connotations aren't necessarily unwarranted. A recent report from Oxford Economics projected that 20 million manufacturing jobs worldwide will be lost by 2030 as a result of automation.[8] Naturally, many have speculated about how automation on our roadways will affect workers. What will happen to truck drivers, taxi or ride-share drivers, and others employed in transportation and commercial sectors? Researchers estimate that nearly 4 million of these jobs will be displaced over the next thirty years as a result of AVs.[9] And while some believe that growth in other sectors will counteract these losses, it's unclear how easily those directly affected will be able to make the transition. Experts gathered at this year's Urban Forum were in agreement that AVs will eventually lead to a mass restructuring of the US employment landscape, with commercial and transportation sectors being particularly vulnerable to job displacement in the coming decades. Speakers and panelists discussed these and other challenges AVs pose to the job market and discussed policy interventions, such as job–training programs, that could help ease what may prove to be a difficult transition.

As is often the case with technological advancements in the workplace, the potential losses of workers will likely translate into mass gains in efficiency for employers. Contained work sites that are beginning to implement AVs have already begun to demonstrate the potential for streamlining operations. Joe Buckner of Autonomous Stuff has seen firsthand how automated Caterpillar machinery has improved efficiency at mining sites by roughly 20 percent. Engineers are eager to mimic these gains in efficiencies across industries. Jimmy Lanigan and Dan Zakula from Mi-Jack Products are particularly interested in AVs' potential to cut down on bottlenecks and pinch points in the movement of goods. Mi-Jack Products manufactures gantry cranes, which help facilitate the movement of containers at intermodal terminals. The company has recently started to experiment with semiautonomous technology that helps their clients cut down on collisions and track the locations of goods, for example. They see the potential to further improve efficiencies between intermodal facilities by using AVs. Lanigan imagines fleets of autonomous trucks that are able to transport freight at off-peak hours, resulting in increased efficiency not only for his clients but also for commuters, who will no longer have to contend with freight traffic during rush hour. John Baczek, Engineer of Program Development at the Illinois Department of Transportation (IDOT), believes that Illinois is particularly well suited to experiment with using AVs to move goods between intermodal terminals, a step that he expects will pave the way for implementing AV technology on longer-haul freight trips. It comes as no surprise, then, that truckers will likely be among the first professions to see their jobs affected by AVs.

Congress recently earmarked funding for the US Department of Transportation to assess the job impacts of AVs on truckers, in particular.[10] While the report had not yet been published at the time of the conference, Fulton stressed that USDOT was working alongside unions on the report in order to ensure that AVs contribute to quality-of-life improvements for truckers rather than detract from their livelihoods. Trucking, and particularly long-haul trucking, is a notoriously tough career. It puts a strain on family life and a strain on overall health—truckers are particularly at risk for a number of health problems such as diabetes and hypertension.[11] This can be particularly difficult on an aging workforce; the majority of workers start trucking late in life as an encore career. While many trucking jobs will likely be displaced, it's also likely that AV will be an answer to some of the difficulties truckers experience. One possibility, according to Fulton, is that automation could improve safety for truckers on the road by cutting down on fatigue-related accidents. In the long term, he envisions fleets of AV trucks being operated remotely by technicians who are then able to return to their families at the end of the night, addressing some of the most difficult aspects of the job as well as the nationwide shortage of truckers.

Others in the transportation industry are also at risk for job displacement. Much has been written about the impact of AV on ride-share drivers.

Ride-share companies have been among the biggest investors in autonomous technology. Their large-scale investments in automation read to some experts as the final gasp of an industry struggling with profitability. After all, Uber's bottom line would look a lot better if drivers were removed from the equation.[12] And transportation workers won't be the only industry to feel the impacts of AVs. Beth Bond, Head of City Development at Bosch, pointed out that there are far fewer components in AVs, so ripple effects will be felt all along the supply chain when AVs are adopted on a large scale. These developments underscore the importance of instituting policies to protect workers.

According to a recent report by Securing America's Future Energy, AVs have the potential to generate nearly $800 billion in annual social and economic benefits by 2050.[13] Although this is an optimistic estimate that takes into account things like environmental benefits and time saved by commuters, most can agree that AVs will be good for the economy. While many jobs will be displaced, many stand to be created. The primary concern of public officials is ensuring that those affected by job displacement will be able to reap some of the benefits. The truck drivers of today probably aren't going to be first in line for the AV technician job at their former employer—at least not without some planning and training.

Private-sector firms also have a vested interest in ensuring that job seekers are prepared for the changes ahead. Who will fill the new positions created by the burgeoning AV sector if no one is trained for them? This concern has led many to invest in job-training programs. Bond said she sees job training as both a public good and a business asset, and Bosch invests in STEAM education programs all over the world. Mi-Jack has beefed up job-training programs for existing personnel in hopes of retaining those employees as their company's needs shift. They've also begun to foster partnerships with local community colleges and technical schools that will offer apprenticeships for five different types of emerging jobs. Nonprofit organizations have also sprung up to help meet the need—for example, Leave No Veteran Behind provides cybersecurity job training to veterans.

Jerry Quandt, director of the Illinois Autonomous Vehicle Association, anticipates that while stakeholders are unified in the importance of job-training programs, one of the biggest challenges ahead will be predicting the specific nature of jobs that the industry will need, which is still very much up for debate. Experts are still unsure how many of the new jobs created will be white-collar, how many will be blue-collar, and how many will be "light blue"—somewhere in between. While new jobs in AV will likely require a lot more engineering expertise, Lanigan said that increases in production may also lead to a resurgence of manufacturing jobs. No matter the outcome, Don DeLoach, cofounder and CEO of Rocket Wagon Venture Studios, is adamant that experts in the field need to adopt a forward-looking perspective: "The answer is not to ask how can we hold on to this. It's not to say, 'Let's make coal great again!' That's stupid on so many levels. The answer is to say: What does this enable us to do? And how does the opportunity shift? And how can we be proactive in terms of looking forward and leveraging this opportunity instead of being afraid of it? We have to think forward."

GRAND THEFT DATA

While the discussion around AVs is often framed as a transportation issue, it is just as much, if not more so, a data issue. In order for AVs to operate safely and effectively, they need to be gathering information about their environment almost constantly. Unsurprisingly, this generates a lot of data, leading experts in the field to question who owns this data, who is able to access it, and how to ensure its security. These matters are far from settled and have far-reaching implications for all stakeholders. AV developers rely on trusted data and its security to ensure the safety of their products and protect their company's intellectual property. Government agencies need to be able to ensure the security and the effective transfer of data in order to guarantee public safety. They also stand to gain a lot from access to the kinds of data these systems generate about commuter patterns and traffic congestion, for example. Speakers and panelists were adamant that future users of these technologies should have a lot of questions about what kind of personal data AVs will collect and how it will be used. Concerns around data, far from being an ancillary discussion, will dictate the viability of AV implementation in the coming years.

While the technology is there to allow AVs to operate in a closed system, Buckner said that the technology necessary for them to operate in an open system is still being refined. When a vehicle goes from a contained work site to public roads, the challenge moves from simply controlling the vehicle to focusing almost entirely on the vehicle's ability to perceive its environment and even to communicate with other elements on the road—other vehicles and traffic signals, for example. Perfecting this technology is the primary challenge of engineers working with autonomous technologies, and getting it right is crucial to ensuring a vehicle's safety. But while sharing informa-tion with other systems is critical, developers who are protective of their intellectual property have concerns about how much information is being shared when a car from their system talks to a car operated by a competitor. How much of a company's intellectual property is being shared with local and federal governments that are communicating with or tracking the positions of vehicles? Bond anticipates that blockchain technology will be instrumental in facilitating and recording data transactions while maintaining security.

In hopes of facilitating collaboration, easing intellectual property concerns, and guaranteeing vehicle safety, USDOT has developed a communication platform using open-source software that can be adapted to "any hardware, vehicle, or control system."[14] Fulton noted that the platform, called the CARMA Platform, is available for anyone to download and use for free on GitHub. Fulton anticipates that USDOT will also expand its use of Spectrum technology in the coming years for new applications on US roadways, which will require AV manufacturers to integrate vehicle-to-everything (V2X) short-range communications services into their production.[15]

In addition to trying to protect their own intellectual property in their day-to-day operations, AV developers are acutely aware of the threat of cyberattack. Buckner sees hacking as a very real threat. While the internet has been pretty unfazed by security breaches, the risks associated with robotics are much higher. The auto industry is already dealing with this problem, to a lesser extent, with car repairs. Although many malfunctions are software issues that could ostensibly be repaired remotely, DeLoach said that most dealerships still require customers to bring the car into the shop to be repaired because the dealership is worried about its system getting hacked. DeLoach sees closed-system authentication as one way to make intersystems transactions more secure, but he anticipates that internal cybersecurity teams will be standard fixtures at AV companies—and indeed all major businesses—in the future.

In addition to compromising the safety of AVs, security breaches would likely compromise the privacy of AV users. Bosch has recently conducted research studies around the world to assess the "technology readiness" of different companies. According to Bond, the attitudes and priorities of countries and regions vary widely. While privacy is a huge concern in Europe, for example, most US companies prioritize safety and convenience. Bond cautions younger generations who are accustomed to sharing lots of personal information on social media to be more intentional about the data they share and more aware of the potential consequences. In order to satisfy different levels of comfort with technology, Buckner imagines a menu displaying terms of service each time a new user enters an autonomous car, giving the consumer the ability to opt in to various terms that enable different levels of functionality. These considerations on the part of consumers will be particularly important as debates over data access and ownership take shape.

It is impossible to discuss AVs without considering who will own the data this industry uses and generates and who will have access to it moving forward. Although these questions are incredibly important, DeLoach said that people in the industry are just beginning to ask them, and that right now they are making massive assumptions. One of the biggest questions being considered by policymakers is whether cities will be able to access the data that AVs generate. As cities increasingly demand access to data generated by ride-share companies, Bond believes it's fair to expect that they will demand access to data generated by AVs as well. Autonomous vehicles are expected to generate a wealth of data that could help public officials improve travel times and respond to incidents more quickly, for example. A series of "demonstration" grants awarded by USDOT hopes to show how data created by AVs can be used for the public good. For example, the Ohio Department of Transportation was awarded a grant to demonstrate how data can be used to derive insights into mobility and transportation safety in rural areas.[16] Pennsylvania was awarded a grant that will focus on gathering information about AV safety in work zones. Fulton sees the potential to share data from these and other studies with GPS navigation software like Waze to improve safety outcomes. From DeLoach's perspective, collaboration between public-sector and private-sector interests are particularly crucial when it comes to regulating data usage and ownership. He noted that if 99 percent of data is owned by one or two megacompanies, "it's going to create a level of instability on this planet that everyone should be frightened about."

RULES OF THE ROAD

Governing bodies tasked with regulating autonomous and connected vehicle technologies are both figuratively and quite literally planning for a moving target. No one seems to be aligned on when or to what degree this new technology will be implemented, what it will look like, or how it will affect mobility within and between our nation's cities. This uncertainty poses challenges for regulatory bodies tasked with creating policies that ensure the safe, efficient, and equitable implementation of AVs. Policymakers will be challenged to keep up with the breakneck pace of private-sector innovators while planning for an uncertain future. While AVs represent unfamiliar territory for many, planning in the face of rapid change is not an uncommon challenge for public-sector officials. In fact, some see the implementation of AVs as an opportunity for the public and private sectors to collaborate in a way that not only protects the public good but also enhances quality of life.

At the root of the debate about how to regulate AVs is what Leanne Redden, executive director of Chicago's Regional Transit Authority (RTA), describes as a "clash of cultures" between the private and public sectors. Simply put, each party has different priorities and responsibilities. They speak different languages and move at different paces. This has made it difficult to settle on a set of collective goals and has historically forced the public sector to be reactive rather than proactive. That's why Redden and others are adamant that regulatory bodies have an early seat at the table, even if that means the slower implementation of AVs: "I know they think this is laborious and slow, but we can't let complete disruption take over." Many public-sector experts at the 2019 Urban Forum, concerned about the disruptive impact technologies like AVs may have on public good, echoed that sentiment.

The exponential growth of ride-share companies in the past decade is just one example of how innovation has been disruptive to cities. As new transit options become available every day—the scooter being the most recent iteration—Erin Aleman, executive director at the Chicago Metropolitan Agency for Planning (CMAP), believes that technology has never been so disruptive to government. Aleman worries that the private sector, eager to get new innovations to market as quickly as possible, often prioritizes market share over the values government is charged with upholding, such as equity, livability, or community. This disconnect is further complicated by the increased liability of governments to the public. John Yonan, superintendent at the Cook County Department of Transportation and Highways, pointed out that government and regulatory bodies are liable to the public in a way the private sector is not. Yonan suspects that public sector liability will not only delay the process of implementing new policy geared at autonomous technology, it may also make it difficult for developers to determine whom to approach within city governments or how to engage them. Lanigan sees huge potential for the public sector to streamline communication. In anticipation of some of these concerns, Dorval Carter, president of the Chicago Transit Authority (CTA), has created a new Chief Innovation Officer position at CTA that he hopes will help private-sector interests better navigate their internal bureaucracy. Traditional procurement procedures aren't set up to deal with the kind of engagements AVs might require, and increasingly

Carter has found companies approaching CTA looking to partner on less clear-cut, incremental changes or projects like pilot programs. At this point, there are no best practices and little precedent for these kinds of engagements. Government agencies and AV companies alike are looking for some degree of guidance for how to move forward with implementation efforts. But while investors are willing to pour money into developing the technology itself, Carter said, there are not nearly as many resources dedicated to determining how municipalities are going to integrate these technologies as they evolve. Public- and private-sector stakeholders agree that more effort needs to be put into developing the ecosystem within which AVs will operate. As Quandt puts it, cars that drive themselves might be the bright shiny penny, but ultimately the autonomous revolution will be an exercise in collaboration. Pilot programs that have sprouted up across US cities are therefore not just testing grounds for new technology but case studies in public-private partnership.

Currently a few different pilot programs are testing autonomous technology across Illinois, and several more are in the works. One of the biggest piloting partnerships to date is Autonomous Illinois, which is currently running pilot programs of automated and connected technology in Itasca, northeastern Illinois, and Chicago's Bronzeville neighborhood. The partnership, launched by former Illinois governor Bruce Rauner in 2018, brings together various state and municipal agencies as well as private-sector entities like artificial intelligence companies and electric vehicle manufacturers, energy companies, business parks, and real estate development companies.[17] Two of the active pilots involve Innova EV, an electric vehicle manufacturer based in Burr Ridge, Illinois. Innova's fleet of electric "Dash" vehicles are currently being piloted in Bronzeville as a form of transportation for the elderly and as a possible last-mile solution between the Itasca Metra station and the Hamilton Lakes Business Park. Although the Dash vehicles are currently semiautonomous and are piloted by drivers, partners on the project expect this to change in the coming years.[18] A third testing project sponsored by Autonomous Illinois is focused on piloting Level 2 driver assistance and collecting advanced systems performance and roadway data in northeastern Illinois. The initiative is a partnership between Autobon AI, which is developing autopilot technology for the freight industry, and the MSD Express trucking company.[19] Redden has been involved with the pilot in Itasca along with John Baczek, engineer of program development at the Illinois Department of Transportation (IDOT). They believe that this kind of suburban testing environment is most appropriate for autonomous pilot programs. Although contextually different, suburban testing may help determine whether and how AVs could be safely implemented in more complex urban environments. Buckner, from Autonomous Stuff, has also been involved in local piloting programs in Peoria, Illinois, where the company is currently testing its autonomous software. While all of these pilot programs are concerned primarily with vehicle testing, several other local initiatives have sprouted up to answer more complex questions about AVs. For example, a new partnership between DeLoach's Rocket Wagon Ventures and CityTech Collaborative seeks to better understand how various heterogeneous autonomous systems will come together to form an ecosystem that is capable of ensuring safety and efficiency on the roads. While streamlined AV software is certainly part of the picture, the project takes it a step further by imagining the roles cities may also play as operators of their own autonomous systems.

The role of local and federal agencies as operators hasn't been discussed nearly as much as their role as regulators, but AV experts are in agreement that agencies will likely need to operate their own autonomous infrastructure and transportation systems in the future. One local early iteration of such a system is the Illinois Tollway's SmartRoad pilot, which gathers real-time data about road conditions and communicates them with drivers along the road.[20] Aimee Lee, senior manager of strategic planning and programming at Illinois Tollway, said that the pilot has helped improve travel times by maximizing the pavement available on the tollway and has been relatively cheap to implement, costing only $100,000 to implement over a sixteen-mile stretch. This is welcome news for public agencies concerned about the costs of infrastructure improvements associated with AVs. With the existing infrastructure in a state of disrepair across the nation—the American Society of Civil Engineers estimates that the United States is in need of roughly $4.59 trillion in infrastructure repairs[21]—investing in autonomous systems feels out of reach for many cash-strapped cities. Finding the money to simply update and maintain roadways to make AV use safer may prove difficult enough, as AV developers eagerly look to public agencies for infrastructure improvements like clear lane markings that many autonomous systems currently rely on to function properly. Buckner said that working infrastructure is something AV developers can plan for to a degree, but improvements will be necessary to ensure that AVs can operate as safely and efficiently as possible.

In this sense, the current state of infrastructure presents an opportunity to bring roadways and transit systems into the future. According to Fulton, some of USDOT's demonstration grants are focused on assessing how vehicles operate in imperfect circumstances—without perfect infrastructure, or in bad weather, for example. The hope is that AVs can be introduced while infrastructure is allowed to catch up incrementally. The incremental changes cities have made in the wake of the Americans with Disabilities Act of 1990 may serve as one model for how to make gradual infrastructure improvements. Rather that infrastructure being replaced all at once, features may be updated over time to be compliant with the latest technology and regulations. In Illinois, Baczek said, the 2019 gas tax increase puts IDOT in a better position to begin making improvements as they make sense. Lee sees opportunities to save money as a result of AV implementation as well and anticipates being able to eliminate certain elements, like gantries on highways today, that may not be required on the roadways of the future, saving hundreds of thousands in maintenance and repairs. Lee also sees the opportunity to offset the costs of investing in new infrastructure by outsourcing those costs to private-sector partners that are eager to see roadways repaired to their standards. At the same time, Lee said, public-sector officials will need to be cautious about implementing new systems too quickly—given the speedy pace of AV innovation, it could be a huge cost to prematurely adopt technology only to see it become obsolete a few years down the road.

In addition to implementing autonomous technology as part of roadway infrastructure, there has been speculation about how cities might incorporate automation into public transit systems. Metra has already begun to incorporate positive train control into their systems to act as a safety measure in case anything happens to the engineer during service.[22] Carter sees the potential to implement semiautonomous technology at the Chicago Transit Authority (CTA) but believes the technology hasn't yet reached a point where this would be practical. He's also concerned about how customers would respond to this kind of technology, particularly on CTA trains. On crowded trains or buses, engineers or drivers serve a greater purpose than merely piloting the vehicle—they have a variety of responsibilities including addressing problems that arise and responding in the event of an emergency. This makes a future with driverless CTA trains and buses seem far fetched to Carter, who is more interested in how AVs can work together with existing public transit infrastructure to expand mobility options across the city. Right now the Chicago transit system, like most transit systems, relies heavily on passengers to piece together different modes of transportation to get to where they need to go. In the future, he imagines a seamlessly integrated system that allows different modes of transportation to work together proactively and respond to passengers' varied needs—a system that builds on the transit resources already in place.

On the other side of this coin, of course, is the fear that AVs will effectively displace other modes of transit, causing all manner of concerns including increased congestion, pollution, and social isolation. Redden is concerned that if AVs are not properly regulated, they will disrupt current transportation modes in the city's urban core. This is something cities have already experienced to a lesser extent with the rapid implementation of ride-share services and scooters. Aleman is adamant that AVs need to enhance rather than devalue public transit systems. In this sense, regulation goes beyond ensuring safety and becomes about creating a regulatory environment that minimizes the potential negative outcomes and maximizes the potential benefits. The National Association of City Transportation Officials has created a blueprint to answer some of the questions many public officials have about how AVs advance the social, economic, and environmental goals of municipalities.[23] The second edition of the Blueprint for Autonomous Urbanism advises cities on how AVs might affect existing transit, how to price AVs to minimize congestion and promote equity, how to manage the onslaught of data, how to regulate urban freight, and how AVs stand to affect urban design.

Congestion is a front-of-mind concern for many transit agencies. If AVs supplant public transportation systems as a primary mode of transportation within Chicago's central business district and the immediate surrounding areas, the increased traffic will make it nearly impossible to get around. The population of high-rise developments in this area is too dense. Carter used Willis Tower as an example. If all the residents of Willis Tower alone decided to take solo AVs to work, he estimates that it would take them seven hours to get to their offices in the morning—not exactly efficient transportation. Also, if AVs continuously roam the streets rather than parking, it will drastically increase the number of cars on the road. To disincentivize these sorts of behaviors and to help fund infrastructure improvement, Aleman said, CMAP plans to implement congestion pricing in certain parts of the city and is considering the possibility of creating AV-dedicated highway lanes to help cut down on traffic. If these issues are adequately regulated, professionals hope that AVs may actually help improve congestion on roads by increasing efficiency and preventing bottlenecks on highways.

Closely related to congestion is pollution—the more cars on the road, the more emissions are leaked into the atmosphere. With many cities implementing sustainability plans to address climate change, minimizing emissions has become increasingly important, leading many experts to call for mandates that require AVs to be fully electric. ACES, which stands for *autonomous, connected, electric, shared*, has become the rallying cry of experts concerned about possible negative outcomes of AVs. Without necessary regulations in place, experts like Dan Sperling, who published a book in 2018 about AV implementation titled *Three Revolutions: Steering Automated, Shared, and Electric Vehicles to a Better Future*, believe that the market may be slow to transition to electric vehicles. Of course, transitioning to electric vehicles will also require infrastructure improvements and up-front investments in facilities such as charging stations that will make electric vehicles more feasible. According to Fulton, USDOT is working together with the Department of Energy on federal policy that is focused on researching battery systems and reducing emissions. Perhaps unexpectedly, many AV developers have been receptive to the idea of electric cars, as many components of autonomous cars already require electricity to operate effectively.

Cities like Chicago that already struggle with transit inequities need to be particularly thoughtful to ensure that AVs are implemented in an equitable manner. Aleman is concerned about the perception that public transit is primarily used by low-income residents and is adamant that AVs be accessible to low-income folks. Carter is also concerned that a reduction in social interactions that take place in the public realm, and on public transit in particular, might socially isolate city residents in a way that is not beneficial to the public good. The image of hoards of isolated passengers in their AVs commuting to work without interacting with anyone outside of their social circle seems poised to further divide residents across racial and class lines. Carter is hesitant to usher in a new urban reality that produces this kind of environment. Autonomous vehicles also likely have the power to either reinforce or combat existing inequities based on how their economic impacts are distributed and shared across demographics and geographies. If harnessed correctly, AVs may represent a huge opportunity to spur economic development in struggling regions. Aleman said that CMAP is starting to think about how the Chicago region can be more strategic about guiding investment to areas in need. Rantoul, Illinois, where an AV testing track has been proposed, may become a case study for this type of guided investment. The proposed test track at the Illinois Center for Transportation is being considered in partnership with the Smart Transportation Infrastructure Initiative, a consortium of universities and research institutes, including the University of Illinois at Chicago and its Urban Transportation Center.[24] Already it has captured the interest of outside investors including Amazon, Uber, Verizon, and Google—an exciting prospect for a city that is currently struggling with above-average levels of unemployment and poverty.[25]

While the federal government will be primarily responsible for implementing safety standards for AVs, Fulton said that this is essentially where their purview ends. This poses another challenge in regulating autonomous technology—how to decide which agencies regulate what. John Yonan, superintendent of the Cook County Department of Transportation and Highways, said that while the state government dictates the rules of the road, local counties and municipalities often must be aligned on policies. Aleman believes that CMAP is particularly well positioned to create unified policy on AVs for the Chicago metropolitan area and act as a thought leader in guiding AV policy in the years ahead.

THE PASSENGER

While speakers and panelists primarily discussed the nuts and bolts of AV development and implementation, the subtext of the discussion was clear—AVs will change the way we think about mobility. Routines and lifestyles will change. Commutes and how we think about work will shift. We will need to reimagine how we organize space in our cities. As a nation that has produced a whole lexicon of cultural touchstones referencing not just the automobile but the act of driving itself, some have even speculated that the advent of self-driving cars is antithetical to aspects of Americans' sense of collective identity.[26]

Quandt knows that autonomous technology is not just a transportation issue. More broadly, we must consider technology's impact on society. Because it signals sweeping changes in the way people and things move around, discussions about AVs can easily become emotionally charged, prompting feelings of anxiety, hope, and fear. It's difficult not to talk about AVs, then, without getting a little dreamy. During her keynote address, Aleman imagined a future in which her children won't ever need to learn how to operate a vehicle in the same way. There are lots of little moments, like the first time your parent lets you drive the car, that likely won't have the same cultural significance in the future. Aimless road trips with ambling stops at roadside attractions or detours along the scenic route may also become a thing of the past or, even more interestingly, go the way of the typewriter, with nostalgia seekers paying a premium to rent vintage cars and experience the freedom of the open road.

Much has been said about the impact of self-driving cars on employment, but less considered is the potential of AVs to affect work culture and work-life balance. Aleman noted that AVs could significantly improve some long commutes. If vehicle users do not need to focus on the road, Aleman sees the opportunity to cut down on time away from home by allowing some employees to leave the workplace earlier and finish out their work day on the way home. Of course, this could present the opportunity for net losses in quality of life if workers are pressured to spend more hours of the day plugged into work. If long commutes become less painful, AVs could also have the unintended consequence of incentivizing employees to relocate further away from their jobs, leading to sprawl. Aleman said that planners will be tasked with anticipating and adapting regulations to prevent these and other unintended consequences.

But while some have asserted that AVs will lead to the loss of the actual (and metaphysical) freedom that comes from being behind the wheel of a car, several demographics stand to uniquely benefit from AVs: the elderly, people with disabilities, children, and caretakers. Fulton is working with the disability community at USDOT to ensure that members of the community are able to take advantage of the new technology in ways that benefit their quality of life. The Dash pilot program in Bronzeville hopes to explore how AVs might be similarly beneficial to elderly populations. As people age and are no longer able to drive, those without access to or the ability to easily take public transportation become cut off from their social circles and often must rely on others to assist with errands. Autonomous vehicles offer to give them back a measure of independence. Redden is hopeful that these benefits might also extend to children and parents. With the price of child care skyrocketing in cities, AVs have the potential to open up child care possibilities for busy working parents. Redden imagines AVs expanding workday child care options available to parents or lending a helping hand transporting children between home, school, and after-school activities.

CONCLUSION

Like most technological advances to date, AVs have been introduced with promises to improve all manner of social ills. Although it's tempting to indulge these idealistic visions of tomorrow, it's important to recognize that AVs likely will not usher in a new urban utopia. The reality is much more complicated, and we know this because the future that is being discussed has already arrived.

Each year the Future City Competition asks middle school students from across the country to imagine the city of the future. The nationwide program is designed to get sixth-, seventh-, and eighth-grade students excited about

STEM fields.[27] Recently, John Yonan, superintendent of the Cook County Department of Transportation and Highways and a volunteer judge for the competition, has noticed an interesting trend: students have started to design their models of cities without roads or highways. At least not the same kinds of roads and highways that many of us are used to driving on today. With the internet abuzz each week about the latest self-driving car release and innovation, these students offer a gentle reminder that the future is not something on the horizon but something we must plan for today.

Notes

1. Paul Lienert and Maria Caspani, "Americans Still Don't Trust Self-Driving Cars, Reuters/Ipsos Poll Finds," *Reuters*, April 1, 2019, www.reuters.com/article/us-autos-selfdriving-poll/americans-still-dont-trust-self-driving-cars-reuters-ipsos-poll-finds-idUSKCN1RD2QS.

2. National Highway Traffic Safety Administration, "A Drive through Time," https://one.nhtsa.gov/nhtsa/timeline/index.html.

3. Alexis C. Madrigal, "7 Arguments against the Autonomous Vehicle Utopia," *The Atlantic*, December 20, 2018, www.theatlantic.com/technology/archive/2018/12/7-arguments-against-the-autonomous-vehicle-utopia/578638.

4. Center for Sustainable Systems, University of Michigan, "Autonomous Vehicles Factsheet," Pub. No. CSS16-18 (2019).

5. Zeninjor Enwemka, "Consumers Don't Really Want Self-Driving Cars, MIT Study Finds," WBUR: Bostonomix, May 25, 2017, www.wbur.org/bostonomix/2017/05/25/mit-study-self-driving-cars.

6. Tory Griggs and Daisuke Wakabayashi, "How a Self-Driving Uber Killed a Pedestrian in Arizona," *New York Times*, March 21, 2018, www.nytimes.com/interactive/2018/03/20/us/self-driving-uber-pedestrian-killed.html.

7. Hannah Knowles, "Uber's Self-Driving Cars Have a Huge Flaw When It Comes to Jaywalkers," *Washington Post*, November 8, 2019, www.sciencealert.com/investigation-reveals-uber-s-self-driving-cars-weren-t-programmed-for-jaywalkers.

8. Rory Cellan-Jones, "Robots 'to Replace up to 20 million factory jobs' by 2030," *BBC News*, June 26, 2019, www.bbc.com/news/business-48760799.

9. Securing America's Future Energy (SAFE), "How and When Will Autonomous Vehicles Impact the Workforce?," https://avworkforce.secureenergy.org/workforce.

10. U.S. Department of Transportation. "Impact of Autonomous Vehicle Technologies on Workforce," December 10, 2019, www.transportation.gov/av/workforce.

11. The National Institute for Occupational Safety and Health, "Long-Haul Truck Drivers," Center for Disease Control and Prevention, March 13, 2018, www.cdc.gov/niosh/topics/truck/health.html.

12. Alexis C. Madrigal, "7 Arguments against the Autonomous Vehicle Utopia," *The Atlantic*, December 20, 2018, www.theatlantic.com/technology/archive/2018/12/7-arguments-against-the-autonomous-vehicle-utopia/578638.

13. Securing America's Future Energy (SAFE), "How and When Will Autonomous Vehicles Impact the Workforce?"

14. U.S. Department of Transportation, "Cooperative Driving Automation," US-DOT, Federal Highway Administration, December 2, 2019, https://cms7.fhwa.dot.gov/research/research-programs/operations/carma-overview.

15. U.S. Department of Transportation, "Future Spectrum Requirements: An Analysis of Transportation Spectrum Needs 2019 through 2033," USDOT, April 2019, www.transportation.gov/sites/dot.gov/files/docs/pnt/341326/dot-future-spectrum-requirements-documentfinalacc.pdf.

16. Ohio Department of Transportation, "D.A.T.A. in Ohio: Deploying Automated Technology Anywhere," DriveOhio, March 21, 2019, www.transportation.gov/sites/dot.gov/files/docs/policy-initiatives/automated-vehicles/351456/35-odot.pdf.

17. Illinois Department of Transportation, "IDOT 2018 Annual Report," 2018, www.idot.illinois.gov/Assets/uploads/files/About-IDOT/Reports/2018_IDOT_Annual_Report.pdf.

18. Stacey Baca, "Illinois Launches Pilot Program for Autonomous Vehicles," ABC 7 Chicago, October, 25, 2018, https://abc7chicago.com/technology/illinois-launches-pilot-program-for-autonomous-vehicles/4555642.

19. Illinois Department of Transportation, "IDOT 2018 Annual Report."

20. Illinois Tollway, "SmartRoad," August 30, 2017, www.illinoistollway.com/documents/20184/582259/SmartRoad+One+Pager.pdf/102f501d-e64b-4f80-8797-ecbb98a241c8.

21. American Society of Civil Engineers, "ASCE's 2017 Infrastructure Report Card: America's Infrastructure Scores a D+," www.infrastructurereportcard.org.

22. Metra, "Positive Train Control," https://metrarail.com/riding-metra/safety-environmental-compliance/positive-train-control-ptc.

23. National Association of City Transportation Officials, "Blueprint of Autonomous Urbanism: Second Edition," https://nacto.org/publication/bau2.

24. University of Illinois at Urbana-Champaign, Smart Transportation Infrastructure Initiative, https://stii.illinois.edu.

25. Dave Hinton, "Test Track Would Be Major Shot in the Arm for Rantoul Economy," *Rantoul Press*, April 12, 2019, www.rantoulpress.com/news/test-track-would-be-major-shot-in-arm-for-rantoul/article_7155cdee-5d5c-11e9-9d50-173a300a971d.html.

26. Robert Moor, "What Happens to the American Myth When You Take the Driver Out of It?" *New York Magazine*, October 17, 2016, http://nymag.com/intelligencer/2016/10/is-the-self-driving-car-un-american.html.

27. DiscoverE and National Engineers Week Future City Competition, "What Is Future City?," https://futurecity.org/about.

Contributors

AUSTIN BROWN is executive director of the Policy Institute of Energy, Environment and the Economy at the University of California Davis, where he builds strong connections between the research and policy communities at the local, state, and national levels with a focus on clean energy and sustainable transportation. Prior to joining UC Davis in June 2017, he spent nine years in Washington, DC, working for the Department of Energy, the National Renewable Energy Laboratory, and as Assistant Director for Clean Energy and Transportation at the White House Office of Science and Technology Policy in the Obama administration. He holds a BS from Harvey Mudd College and a PhD from Stanford University.

STAN CALDWELL is an adjunct associate professor of transportation and public policy at the Heinz College of Information Systems and Public Policy at Carnegie Mellon University. He teaches courses in intelligent transportation systems and advises student projects related to transportation. Stan also serves as executive director of Carnegie Mellon's Traffic21 Institute, which is housed in the Heinz College, and executive director of the USDOT-designated Mobility21 National University Transportation Center, which is housed in the College of Engineering. Stan conducts research in policy related to disruptive new technologies, including connected and automated vehicles. He serves on the Leadership Circle of the Intelligent Transportation Society of America and curates the industry-recognized Traffic21 Smart Transportation Dispatch. He also serves as a founding member of the Pennsylvania Autonomous Vehicle Policy Task Force, the State Transportation and Innovation Council, and the Smart Belt Coalition.

CHRIS HENDRICKSON is the Hamerschlag University Professor Emeritus and director of the Traffic21 Institute at Carnegie Mellon University, a member of the National Academy of Engineering, editor-in-chief of the *ASCE Journal of Transportation Engineering,* and chair of the Transportation Research Board Division of the National Research Council. His research, teaching, and consulting are in the general area of engineering planning and management, including design for the environment, system performance, construction project management, finance, and computer applications. Hendrickson pioneered models of dynamic traffic equilibrium, including time-of-day departure demand models. He has worked on green design, exploring the environmental life-cycle consequences of alternative product and process designs, especially for alternative fuels.

KAZUYA KAWAMURA is a professor at the Department of Urban Planning and Policy at the University of Illinois at Chicago. He also holds a courtesy appointment at the Department of Civil and Materials Engineering. He has over one hundred publications on a variety of topics, including transport economics, travel analysis, and urban freight planning and policies. He holds a BS degree in mechanical engineering from the North Carolina State University, Raleigh, and PhD and master's degrees in civil engineering from the University of California, Berkeley.

TAYLOR LONG is a writer and urban planner living in Chicago. Taylor strives to connect meaningfully with communities, promote equitable development, and preserve sense of place in our cities. She has worked to map cultural assets in Chicago, consulted on regional affordable housing initiatives, and conducted research on sustainable travel, postindustrial redevelopment, and small business retention. She writes about cities and travel for various publications. She holds a master's degree in urban planning and public affairs from the University of Illinois at Chicago.

MICHAEL A. PAGANO is dean of the College of Urban Planning and Public Affairs at the University of Illinois at Chicago, director of UIC's Government Finance Research Center, professor of public administration, former coeditor of *Urban Affairs Review* (2001–14), and nonresident senior fellow of the Brookings Institution's Metropolitan Policy Program. He has published ten books, including *Metropolitan Resilience in a Time of Economic Turmoil, Terra Incognita, Cityscapes and Capital,* and *The Dynamics of Federalism,* and more than one hundred publications on urban finance, capital budgeting, federalism, infrastructure, urban development, and fiscal policy. Since 1991 he has written the annual *City Fiscal Conditions* report for the National League of Cities and recently published a Brookings report summarizing a multiyear project on fiscal policy space at www.brookings.edu/research/city-budgets -in-an-era-of-increased-uncertainty.

P. S. SRIRAJ   heads the Urban Transportation Center at UIC, which is dedicated to conducting research, inspiring education, and providing technical assistance on urban transportation planning, policy, operations, and management. As a researcher, he has focused on public transportation systems, sustainability and transportation, and visualization of transportation. His broad experience includes using data and information systems to address complex urban issues, particularly in the areas of stakeholder involvement and other socioeconomic factors in transportation planning. Sriraj has led projects totaling more than $6 million supporting research on the operations and planning of surface transportation.

The University of Illinois Press
is a founding member of the
Association of American University Presses.

University of Illinois Press
1325 South Oak Street
Champaign, IL 61820-6903
www.press.uillinois.edu